Thinking It Through:
A Practical Guide to Academic Essay Writing

Third Edition

Martin Boyne
Mary Ann Armstrong
Maged El Komos

Heather Avery
Lucille Strath
Karen Taylor
Kathleen James-Ca\

D1367646

Academic Skills Centre
Trent University
Peterborough, 2005

Thinking It Through: A Practical Guide to Academic Essay Writing

Academic Skills Centre
Trent University, Peterborough, Ontario K9J 7B8

Printed in Canada by Richard's Printing

Permissions Granted

National Post. February 18, 2004. Material reproduced on pages 71-74 of this text by permission.

EBSCOhost. Screen capture reproduced on page 47 of this text by permission.

Canadian Cataloguing in Publication Data

Thinking it through

3rd ed.
ISBN 1-894674-33-2

1. Essay. 2. Exposition (Rhetoric). 3. English language-Rhetoric.
I. Avery, Heather. II Trent University. Academic Skills Centre.

PE1471.T55 1989   808'.042   C89-094813-5

Table of Contents

List of Exercises and Checklists

Exercises

Checklists

Preface

THIS THIRD EDITION of *Thinking It Through* draws on the success of the previous editions of the book by preserving much of both the structure and the content. Users of those editions will thus be pleased to find that they need not spend time reacquainting themselves with the layout of the new edition. So what, exactly, is "new"?

First, we are pleased to follow the lead of our other flagship publication, *Notes on the Preparation of Essays*, by moving to a lie-flat spiral binding. This will make reading and referring to the book, not to mention teaching and learning from it, much easier. Second, since much has changed in the area of technology since the revised edition of *Thinking It Through* was published in 1995, we have revised many of the chapters to acknowledge that essay writing now takes place more commonly with keyboards and word-processing packages than with fingers and index cards; in particular, the chapters on research, notetaking, and drafting have been "thought through" anew with this in mind. That said, in the spirit of the revised second edition, we do not neglect traditional approaches to writing, realizing that many students still benefit greatly from writing longhand, conducting research in library stacks, and spreading their notes over their bedroom floor. Our most recent revisions, in fact, alert essay writers to the dangers of relying too heavily on technology: we see it as a tool to help students write, not as a force that controls their writing.

Elsewhere, we have tried to freshen some of our examples and exercises to reflect more recent times. While we remember the 1970s and 1980s quite well, we know that many of our readers do not; analogies and references that are meaningful are always more successful. We have also added exercises and checklists in various places (and have included handy lists of these at the front of the book). The sample essays are also new, not because we found fault with the old ones, but because we know how helpful it can be for teachers to use fresh essays in their classes; the essays were written quite recently and in two cases contain quite up-to-date theories, research, and references.

So, while the book has come a long way since its first inception twenty-five years ago, its central philosophy remains the same. This philosophy, described in detail in Chapter 1, gives rise to the healthy imbalance between preparation (Chapters 2-6) and actual writing (Chapter 7) that is, we feel, one of the strengths of our approach to the task of essay writing. We owe much in this regard to those who compiled the original manual that would become *Thinking It Through*: Peter Slade, Richard Harrison, Isobel Henniger, Kari Lie, and Sheree-Lee Powsey. Peter Slade deserves special recognition, since it was he who wrote most of the material (for a short course in essay writing) that was transformed in the summer of 1987 into the first edition of this book. The influence of those responsible for the transformation — Catherine Taylor, Annette Tromly, and Stephen Brown — continues into this new edition; their work even yet, in the words of the preface to the second edition, "provides the backbone" of what you see in this edition.

The crafters of the second edition deserve our thanks, too: Heather Avery, Lucille Strath, Karen Taylor, and Kathleen James-Cavan. Heather, Lucille, and Karen served as friends and mentors to all of us at some point during our early years at the Centre (and beyond), and it is from them that we learned the art of collaborative writing that has endured into this new edition.

This book has a rather symbiotic relationship with the core teaching of the Academic Skills Centre: we use the material in these pages in our individual conferences and workshop sessions, and in turn that teaching helps us to adapt and improve the advice and strategies proposed in *Thinking It Through*. We must, therefore, acknowledge the crucial but often unseen role that our own students play in all of our publications. In particular, of course, we thank those students whose words appear in the book, either through examples or in the new sample essays in Appendix D. Finally, we are all grateful for the dedication to this enormous task of Deb Nichols, the Centre's publications coordinator. She nurtured this edition from the beginning: from planning to design, from editing to proofreading, and — to her great relief — through to its ultimate appearance in print.

As we can all attest, the creative process is all about starts and restarts, about building on some ideas and rejecting others; in the end, we trust that you, the reader, will benefit as much from thinking through this process as we have.

1 The Essay: Thinking It Through

DOES LIFE OFFER the student any prospect more daunting than the nasty gloom of deadlines? Surely the long essay is the most bullying of all professorial designs, deliberately contrived, so it seems, first to exasperate and finally to humiliate the student. Essay writing is very much an ordeal, unnatural in certain senses and always painful in the execution because it is a challenge to single combat, an exercise that demands self-commitment and fails without self-control. To begin to write is difficult, to persist exhausting; to conclude requires a spry wit and a fresh mind when you are least likely to possess either.

All kinds of work take their toll on the worker. But the peculiar stress that afflicts the writer comes not only from the outside forces of the assignment itself — the fear of not meeting the deadline, of falling in the professor's esteem, of failing the essay and then the course and as a result losing the A average required to get into law school — but also from the inward motions of self-discovery. The essay is inescapably a record of the life of its author, a map of the progress of one mind contemplating some part of the world it inhabits.

While the outside forces of deadlines do produce anxiety, the inward motions of self-discovery bring a deep sense of satisfaction. That pain and joy are inextricably entwined is one of life's paradoxes. The all-consuming nature of essay writing is the very thing that allows you to see beyond the ordinary and to measure the personal gains made by finally fixing on a page the new dimensions of what you think and know. Yes, it is hard work, but it is hard pleasurable work. The sense of accomplishment that comes from taking on the challenge of close research and communicating its results far exceeds all the difficulties you may have had.

History of the Essay

It is from the tradition of an individual thinking something through that the academic essay springs. The rise of the essay in European culture in the late sixteenth century was coincidental with the evolution of the notion of individual freedom and the increased recognition of the value of the self. For Montaigne and Francis Bacon, both as humanists and scientists (for neither man would have distinguished between the humanities and the sciences as we do), the essay was an explorative kind of writing — a laboratory of words, if you like. Montaigne named the new species from the French *essayer* ("to attempt"), and he first assayed topics ranging from politics to theology, from cannibals to reflections on solitude, death, and marriage. Bacon's essays are less preoccupied with the inward explorations of his own mind than are those of Montaigne, and they are given more to the examination of the outer world of nature in all its measurable and observable variety; he was, not surprisingly, the developer of the scientific method.

For both men the essay was the private voice of public experience, a personal and original mode of argumentation. Not only was the form of the essay new, but the use of prose was itself a fledgling endeavour in English. Prose writing encouraged a particularly personal spoken rhythm that lacked the formal restraints of metre and rhyme through which poems were written. It was more natural and less preconceived than poetry. The essay thus began as the simplest and most naturally reflective, self-generating, and self-sustaining kind of prose. With the development of the periodical or journal essay and the rise of eighteenth-century prose stylists like Addison, Johnson, and Goldsmith, the essay became more widely public in its audience. The need for an objective voice and the difficulty of sustaining distance from one's own text became more prominent concerns of the essayist. The tone of the nineteenth-century essayist is discreetly public, and we seldom encounter an eccentrically private voice like that of Swift's Bickerstaff.

Still, the finest modern essayists, such as George Orwell, while managing to sustain a respectfully objective distance from the topic, have recognizable voices. Their private voices are addressed to a public audience in a way that does not permit the wandering off into the merely personal terrain of feelings, tastes, prejudices, and other autobiographical details. Yet, although the word "I" might not appear extensively in it, the modern essay is personal: while the author may address the many, he or she remains only one individual talking. Whether that of the scientist or of the humanist, the language of the essayist is always and intimately expressive, a distinctly personal use of language generated by the unique unfolding of the idea pursued, more or less successfully, in each single exercise of writing. Essay writing is the art of channelling a private inner conversation between the mind and its subject into a public outer form, so that all essayists can say with Montaigne, "I am the text of my own book."[1]

The Academic Essay

Essays have become the primary means by which the community of scholars communicates. University professors, scientific researchers, practising lawyers and physicians, all publish essays in the journals of their own disciplines. Through the essay as journal article, scholars share their research findings, the results of their investigations, new ways of thinking about a subject that accommodate new evidence, and so on. In this way, they help to fulfill one of the primary functions of the university: to advance the growth of knowledge and understanding throughout the world community of scholars.

Clearly then, it is important that career academics learn to write essays well. But what is the point of imposing the burden on the vast majority of students who will become neither professors nor other publishing professionals? The answer lies in another of the overall aims of the academy: to teach students to think. The exercise of writing an essay provides the student with the best and most prolonged opportunity to think deeply and precisely into a subject; it also provides the professor with evidence of the student's ability to think. Essays are so important that students working for a B.A. may have to write as many as forty-five before receiving their degrees.

So what is a good university essay?

Many university students mistakenly think that the aim of university is to learn *things*, to acquire knowledge, to assimilate lots of information. That goal, taken to the extreme, would be dreary and self-defeating. Universities have been in operation for about eight hundred years now, and with the information explosion of our own electronic age, even the most modest university library provides more information than you could read if you outlived Methuselah. The goal, then, is not to devour the library's holdings in your particular discipline, but to develop your analytical ability so that no matter what topic you have in mind, you will be able to think your way into it and bring back something valuable.

[1]Michel de Montaigne, *Essays and Selected Writings*, ed. Donald M. Frame (New York: St. Martin's, 1963) 2.

You will be evaluated not on what you know, but on how well you can think about what you know and on how well your writing elucidates that thought. Your instructors will be looking first for what ideas you can generate, what discriminations you can make, what interpretations you can develop, what arguments you can defend, what conclusions you can draw. These are signs of your ability to think in original and creative ways about the information you encounter. Do not instead set out to tell your reader everything in the world about the parts of the bullfrog or to enumerate every last instance of animal imagery in *Macbeth*. "This and this and this" tend to go in one ear and out the other because there is nothing to hold them all together. Such an attempt ends up in a sort of mail-order catalogue approach: there is an impressive array of merchandise, but the only evidence of order is that all the shoes are in one place and the toasters in another. "So what?" one might say, and the marker frequently does.

What an essay needs and a department store catalogue does not is a governing idea or thesis, some overall insight into the information presented that enables the reader to see how it all fits together. It is in discovering and developing a thesis that you enter the essay, and the instructor will be looking for your presence just as he or she might look for evidence of thorough research. As a writer, then, you must take control. You choose what to emphasize; you look for patterns and relationships emerging and show how your thesis or governing idea casts light on the topic. In some research-based essays, the information will be so prominent that your presence will be difficult to detect; in other papers, the argument is paramount, and your voice, persuading the reader of the soundness of your thesis, will echo throughout. Both kinds of essay, nonetheless, require that the writer remain firmly in control.

While an essay must bear the stamp of its author, its function is to contribute to a scholarly community, to encourage thought and re-examination. The essay thus must reflect self *and* acknowledge audience. A voice in the wilderness cannot be heard unless it is speaking comprehensibly, so, at every stage, the writer must struggle, not only to make meaning, but to make meaning clear.

It is more often lack of confidence than lack of effort that causes essays to go astray. People worry about their own capacities, believing all instructors to have brains more highly evolved than their own. They suppress their own interpretations, spend too much time doing research and not enough time thinking. They settle for the display of acquired knowledge rather than risk the attempt of doing something with it. Ultimately, this safe route is a dead end because it does not lead where you need to go. You must risk the busy expressway — full of construction and detours though it may be. The academic essay is no place to be faint-hearted.

How, then, to ward off the anxiety and self-doubt that make students prefer the cul-de-sac to the bolder path? First, remind yourself that you are in school to learn, that your instructors do not expect undergraduate papers to rival their own scholarly achievements, that if they did, you would be handed a diploma on the first day of your studies, not your last. Remember that writing is often messy, usually difficult, and more difficult some days than others. Take comfort in the assurance that you will get better and more efficient with practice. Work hard, but be as patient with yourself as if you were learning to play the violin.

Second, become methodical in your approach to the task of essay writing. Much of this book is devoted to planning and revising the essay. If you take the time to prepare properly and make the time to revise carefully, your essay will be better and the actual process of writing it will be both faster and less painful. The alternative is to try to perform simultaneously the conflicting feats of forecasting the overall development of the thesis and getting the right emphasis and wording for particular sentences. This task is akin to carving out the shortest route to the heart of the jungle without a map. In that attempt lies much of the dense overgrowth of anxiety, nausea, and wasted paper familiar to those students who skimp on the planning stage of the essay.

The Essay-Writing Process

Over the course of our text we present the various aspects of the essay-writing process. The text commences by tackling the task of working from topic through to thesis. Chapters Three, Four, and Five explore in detail the complexities involved in compiling research and responding to the material accumulated. Chapters Six, Seven, and Eight deal with writing itself: preparing to write, drafting, and revising what has been written. In an appendix, we include the results of this process: three sample essays, one from the humanities, one from the sciences, one from the social sciences. These essays, although good, are not intended to be perfect. They are real undergraduate essays and represent the attempts of their authors to fulfill the demands of the essay. Students can learn from them, not only by using them as models, but also by evaluating them critically.

The process of writing an essay is both telescopic and recursive. It is telescopic in that it begins with a large and rather blurry view of a subject and moves purposefully toward successively more refined and detailed views. Refocusing is required at each shift to a new level of detail. The process is recursive because this continual readjustment means that essay writing does not occur as an uninterrupted sequence of steps. The essayist should be looking for the thesis and trying to forecast the paper from very early in the planning stage, resketching and refining often. Remember that in an essay you are thinking an idea through; the thesis may seem foggy even very late in the writing process. Keep writing and refining until the fog lifts.

2 From Topic to Thesis

The Topic

THE FIRST STEP in writing the essay is finding a topic. Sometimes this is not difficult: the instructor sets the topic for you and says, "Three thousand words before Thanksgiving, please." Other times, you must find your own topic, or narrow a very broad topic, such as "Advertising," into one of more manageable scope, such as "Images of the Female Body in Print Advertising." The topic (from the Greek *topos*) is the "place" you choose to explore in the essay, however you arrive at it. It is the broad field of interest on which you are going to base your research and, hence, your essay.

Choosing a Topic

If a topic has not been assigned by your instructor, be sure to set aside enough time to search for one in the course material. It is wise to determine early in a course how many essays you will be expected to write, whether the topics will be supplied, or if not, what restrictions there are on your choice of topic. The first week of classes is not too early to be thinking about essays you will write later in the semester. When you enrol in a university course, you will have set, no doubt, certain goals for yourself based upon your interests and career plans. Keep these personal goals in mind while looking for topics of particular interest to you which are, also, central to the course you are studying. A good topic is the beginning of every good essay; therefore, select your topic with care.

8

What are the essentials of a good topic?

1. ***The topic interests you.*** You will write more effectively about a subject that engages you intellectually and emotionally. If your topic encompasses a probing question or an issue needing to be resolved, you will be able to generate a thesis or develop an argument more easily. It is challenging. Remember that your essay will differ from others on the basis of interpretations you develop, lines of investigation you pursue, and connections you make. Topics that allow only for restating someone else's research will not be flexible enough to explore in your own way. For instance, a professor may ask you to discuss B.F. Skinner's approach to behavioural psychology. The task, then, is informed by the word "discuss." If you sketch the system of Skinner's thought but offer no critique, you produce a description. A more appropriate reading of the term "discuss" would lead you not only to sketch his system, but also to assess it. Research for your essay should be rewarding; it should add to your store of knowledge. If the material available is old, familiar territory, find a more challenging topic to explore. Finally, do not re-submit one of your papers that has received a grade in another course. The reasons are obvious: no new research has been done, and your efforts have already been marked and rewarded.

2. ***It has enough scope.*** To return to the topic-as-place analogy, is the topic big enough or complex enough to spend two weeks exploring? Or would you end up searching around the same tourist traps on every page in order to fill the required number of words? On the other hand, it should not be too broad. Try to develop a sixth sense for the "fit" of a topic: its appropriateness to the projected length of the essay and to the course objectives. Eagerness to include everything read or heard about a topic often tempts a student to select one that is so wide-ranging that a focused attempt to penetrate below the surface level is impossible. Very broad topics cannot become very deep in the limited space of an essay. An essay is meant to be an in-depth investigation of a topic, not a survey of vast areas of knowledge.

   Sometimes a topic is so intriguing that research for it can go on and on. Try to discipline yourself to fit the task to the time allowed. If you find that a broad, unfocused topic is squandering your time, and all your attempts at focusing it fail, leave it and choose another.

   Consider this topic: The concept of the state from the time of the classical Greeks to the present. Such a topic is much too broad for an essay; this sort of exploration is akin to the tourist-in-a-hurry mentality parodied in the seventies film *If It's Tuesday, This Must Be Belgium.* By trying to cover the world, we miss the significance of the "places" we travel through.

3. ***Adequate research material is available.*** An essay should not require data that you do not have and cannot get. Avoid subjects requiring information that is too specialized. If the required material is likely to be in another language, make sure that you have the skills to translate your material. Before you commit yourself to a topic, and you are unsure about the availability of research material, do a preliminary search.

4. ***It is directed toward the appropriate audience.*** A well-chosen topic will engage the interest and the intellect of instructor and fellow students alike; that is, it will appeal to readers who possess a scholarly level of understanding. You are not writing for the general public, so you should assume a certain shared understanding of the field.

Narrowing the Topic

Sometimes instructors supply only the most general of topics — "modern American poetry"; "organized labour"; "medieval history of Britain"; "human anatomy" — and ask the student to narrow the subject down to appropriate size. To do this you must be mindful of several things: the level of detail at which the course is pitched, the topic's significance within the context of the course, and the projected length of the essay. When an instructor assigns a general topic, she or he does so with the hope that the student will find a suitable subtopic to investigate. If you are at all uncertain of the acceptability of the topic you settle on, check with the instructor. This advice applies to choosing your own topic as well.

It may be helpful to consult reference tools to see how the subject has been divided by other writers:[1]

1. The table of contents and the index in a book on the topic can provide good ideas.

2. The library catalogue system will suggest the natural divisions of broad topics and progressively smaller subtopics, and it will tell you what books the library actually has. There will be a set of volumes located in the catalogue section of the library listing

---

[1]For more information, see Chapter Three on library research.

all the subject headings used in the particular cataloguing system, with subdivisions and cross-reference headings.

3. Journals in the discipline, and indexes to those journals, will indicate what topics others have found interesting and suitable for essay form.

4. Books in the reference section of the library, both general encyclopedias and reference books for a particular discipline, may help you find a topic of interest.

Most important, though, is your own analysis of the topic. Ask yourself a series of questions about the broad topic to reduce it step by step to a manageable size. Look for the stage at which you feel that the topic is neither so broad that it would result in a shallow essay, nor so narrow that it does not catch enough material in its net to develop an adequate thesis. This "feeling" comes largely through practice.

Examples of Narrowed Topics
The first two examples are based on sample essays found in Appendix D.

1. an essay for an international development course

Development, democracy, and human rights
   (What do they mean? Are they related? In what context?)
      Development, democracy, and human rights in the
      new millennium: mutually reinforcing
         (Is this true or is there more to it? Can the
         three be seen in a contrasting way to
         "mutually reinforcing"?)
            Development, democracy, and
            human rights in the new millennium:
            Mutually reinforcing or a cover for
            disempowering market reform?

2. an essay for English literature

Shakespeare's plays
 (all of his plays? too broad)
  Shakespeare's comedies
   (all of them?)
    Shakespeare's *A Midsummer Night's Dream* and *Twelfth Night*
     (similarities between the two? differences?)
      A comparative study of Shakespeare's *A Midsummer Night's Dream* and *Twelfth Night*

3. an essay for environmental studies

Ecology
 Ecological damage
  (in what way? what kind?)
   Ecological damage resulting from fishing
    (where?)
     Ecological damage resulting from fishing in the Otonabee River
      (when?)
       Ecological damage resulting from fishing in the Otonabee River during spawning season

(This one can probably not be narrowed much further without becoming too minute.)

EXERCISE ONE: NARROWING THE TOPIC

Narrow the following topics. Be aware of the questions you formulate to arrive at each level. What is the length of the essay you have in mind? Afterwards, think about what made you decide to stop narrowing when you did. Does the narrowed topic fulfill the requirements of the original broad topic?

1. The Constitutional Rights of Native Peoples

2. The French Revolution

3. Existentialism

4. Bird Migration

Analyzing the Topic

For many well-intentioned students, the first response to a topic either set by an instructor or chosen by themselves is to race to the library, assignment sheet in hand (or worse, at home), and fill their backpacks with whatever books seem somehow relevant. Or they do a Google search on the topic. These students hope that if they read around the topic long enough, clarity will emerge. Research is beneficial at this stage, but before you go too far into your topic, some focusing of your chosen purpose is essential.

Once the topic is narrowed, the next task is to determine exactly what the topic chosen (or assigned) requires you to do. Only then can you really begin thinking about what *you* want to do. If you write a brilliant essay on the nesting habits of the great horned owl when you were asked to discuss its mating habits, you will come to grief at evaluation time.

As soon as you choose or are given a topic, start thinking about the precise nature of the task at hand. Instructors design questions with great care and expect you to notice every aspect of the question you choose: its wording, its emphasis, its inherent structure. Look for the subject of the topic sentence, the articles and phrases that modify nouns, and the verbs that will direct your research action: search for the meaning of the topic. In every case, your aim should be to focus the topic as best you can before going to the library. To "focus the topic" means to see it as a whole and to determine its main or essential points. Focusing requires you to see the topic as a single subject area and also to see the parts that make the whole clear, logical, and understandable. Remember that you need to take control of the essay process early on if you are not to be overwhelmed by unrelated information. The more focused the topic, the more productive your research work will be.

"Analyze" is from the Greek word meaning "to break up." To analyze your topic means, then, to break it up very carefully into its parts so that you can see it more clearly. This is akin to the process that secondary-school students bitterly describe as dissecting a poem and thereby taking the life out of it. Neither a poem nor an essay topic is a science-class frog. If you are careful enough in your analysis, you will be able not only to dissect the topic but to put it back together again, to reassemble it, and to begin to create your essay. You will, in effect, be breathing life back into the topic.

Methods of Analysis

Since topics vary in form, they lend themselves to different methods of analysis. Listed below are several approaches.

1. If the topic is not already in the form of a question, *recast the topic in question form*, specifically in the form of a central question your essay will investigate. Sometimes you can formulate this question very early on; sometimes your preliminary reading will help you find the critical point. Here is an example of how this works. Suppose the topic is this:

    Henry Mintzberg claims that undergraduate students who want to have business careers should not study business at university but should study other subjects such as politics, sociology, philosophy, and literature. Discuss.

Possible questions could be:

*   Do I agree with Henry Mintzberg's claim?
*   Should undergraduate students who want to have business careers not study business at university but study other subjects?
*   What skills do these subjects teach students that the business world would want?

2. *Restate the topic in your own words* to make sure that you understand it. The language that makes deepest sense to you is the language that comes more or less naturally to you. Be careful, though, not to distort or diminish the topic in the translation.

3. *Make sure you understand all the key words and concepts in the question.* Each discipline coins its own words and phrases for

concepts that cannot be specifically and unambiguously expressed by an existing word. These are words like "epistemology," "heuristic," "onomatopoeia," "theodicy," and "structuralism," none of which is likely to pass human lips outside of academic circles. Such words are referred to alternately as "jargon," which means confused, unintelligible language, or as "terminology," which means the system of words that stakes out the milestones and boundaries of a discipline.

In addition, all disciplines employ certain common words in very specialized ways, and it is necessary to be aware of the precise meaning each discipline assigns to a particular word. For example, consider "class" in biology, "organism" in psychology, "scene" in English, "material" in philosophy, "myth" in anthropology. If you use a dictionary frequently (and you should), you will have noticed that many entries have several definitions, some of them keyed to different disciplines, such as medicine, law, or music. You may have to consult specialized reference books such as the *Dictionary of Terms* or course texts to clarify some words and concepts adequately.

See Appendix A for definitions of terms commonly used in essay questions, such as "discuss," "evaluate," and "illustrate." By analyzing these familiar words, you may find the way to begin to interpret the topic.

4. ***Break the topic up into subtopics.*** This approach is invaluable for those eighty-five-word topics that end with the word "discuss." Sometimes such questions begin with the main idea, sometimes the main idea is buried somewhere else in the question, and sometimes the student is expected to deduce the main idea from a series of smaller related ideas. Try rearranging to connect related ideas. Often it is useful to start by copying the question down, beginning a new line for every new sentence. A word of caution here: many students assume that their essays must discuss the ideas presented in the order in which they appear in the question. Not true, and very often not even advisable. Instructors sometimes assign long, complex topics to act as a guide to the several concerns the essay should or could cover.

The four techniques of analyzing a topic discussed so far direct you toward a full understanding of the *topos* or place to be explored. The following three techniques move you right into your essay. The process requires a little imagination. This is the point when you begin to assemble your ideas and make the exact connection between the required task and what is to become your paper.

5. *Try to picture what some or all of the sections might be.* Sit quietly and think about your topic. How will you begin? How will you develop your points? Do you see three major sections, maybe five? Do you see subsections emerging? Conceive the form and contemplate the content of your essay.

   Note that although you may have been taught and become very proficient at the five-paragraph essay, this kind of essay will no longer be appropriate for all your writing assignments. Stop thinking in terms of one point or section equals one paragraph, and three points or sections with an introductory paragraph and a concluding paragraph make an essay. Think in terms of major points or sections and subpoints or subsections. There may be five major sections; there may be two. The form or structure of your essay will develop from your topic, your thesis, your word count, and what you want to say. Start thinking outside the five-paragraph box.

6. If you have been asked to agree or disagree with a statement, ***try to imagine different positions that might be taken***. This thinking process is an important part of all critical analysis. Try constructing lines of argument by which you can defend those positions. Devise a number of possible approaches to your task: the urge to make up one's mind too fast is poisonous to the inquiring intellect. Another very good reason for trying to imagine different positions on a subject is that no matter what position you decide to defend — and you must choose eventually — you will need to know the contrary points of view in order to convince your reader that your argument stands up to apparently and genuinely opposing evidence.

7. *Try brainstorming*. At this stage, you will want to explore your personal store of knowledge of your topic. You may think you know nothing, but you have, in fact, already done some preliminary research. Try to recall information from your notes, lectures, and tutorials. Often you will be surprised by what turns up. Sometimes writing down all the specific ideas that come to mind will take you more deeply into your topic. Afterwards, cull the list, throwing out clearly bird-brained ideas. Look for related ideas that you might cluster together. Then be selective: it is unlikely that everything you have in your list belongs in the same essay. Remember that you cannot do everything in one paper, and for every topic many different and equally appropriate essays are possible.

Checklist: Analyzing the Topic

1. Recast the topic in question form.

2. Restate the topic in your own words.

3. Make sure that you understand all the key words and concepts.

4. Break the topic up into a set of smaller parts.

5. Picture what some or all of the sections of your essay might be.

6. Imagine different positions.

7. Brainstorm.

If you have made a noble attempt to analyze the topic, but you are still feeling a bit uncertain of its precise meaning, ask your instructor for advice. Most instructors are pleased to assist students who are working hard. Finally, remember that some topics are not as well phrased as they might be, and no amount of analysis will wring clarity from an inherently ambiguous or illogical sentence. Again, ask your instructor for assistance in interpreting the topic. Sometimes you have a better grasp on the topic than you think, and just talking about it will allow you to see it more clearly.

EXERCISE TWO: RECASTING THE TOPIC IN QUESTION FORM
What questions suggested by these topics might serve as the central inquiry of an essay?

1. World War I and its impact on the Maritime provinces.

2. The status of Irish immigrants in the United States during the nineteenth century.

3. The locomotive systems of the ant and the fly.

4. Love and fancy in *A Midsummer Night's Dream*.

5. Canada's environmental policies and ozone depletion.

EXERCISE THREE: KEY WORDS AND CONCEPTS
Rephrase the following topics. Then use whatever reference tools are available to find the definitions of the words and concepts used in each question. When you have confidence in the accuracy of your understanding of the topics, rephrase them again. Compare the results with your first attempts.

1. The negative environmental consequences in relation to the economic advantages of the implementation of advanced technology. [course in world development]

2. The commodification of virtue in the modern world. [course in sociology of the workplace]

3. The Treaty of Westphalia (1648) ended the Thirty Years' War and also ended the religious conflicts brought about by the Reformation and Counter-Reformation. [course in European history]

4. Compare the methodological approach of Creighton in his analysis of Canadian settlement patterns with that of Harold Innis in his staples thesis. [course in Canadian studies]

5. *Waiting for Godot* manifests a world view less witty and a thematic reach less ambitious than many plays from the theatre of the absurd. What then accounts for its time-proven power to elicit the affection and attention of theatre audiences? [course in modern drama]

18

EXERCISE FOUR: SUBDIVIDING THE TOPIC

Read the following topics. Analyze each question and decide whether all parts are of equal importance and, if not, which parts should receive more emphasis than others. Are some parts subsections of other parts? What is the overall point of each question? Finish by rewriting the questions, beginning with a statement of the main idea of each.

1. The UN has drawn up a document called the Earth Charter, which was launched at the Hague Peace Palace in June 2000. What is the document's underlying vision of the world and the place of humans in it? What ideologies do you see as influential in it? What obstacles would have to be surmounted and instruments put to work to realize and consolidate this vision? Do you think the Charter will be beneficial to the world?

2. Discuss the social effects of the Industrial Revolution in Britain. How did the society of the Industrial Revolution differ from that which preceded it? Did technological advances change the way people saw their world? Did the new economic arrangements affect interpersonal relations? To what extent does our own society perpetuate the patterns established during the Industrial Revolution?

EXERCISE FIVE: BREAKING UP THE TOPIC

What sections and subsections are suggested by the following topics?

1. Describe and explain the changes in spatial patterns of population in Canada since 1945, and indicate how these changes have affected Canadian cities.

2. Examine the struggles of French Canada for a cultural and political identity distinct from that of the rest of Canada during the period of the Quiet Revolution. Refer to incidents of both violence and cooperation.

EXERCISE SIX: FINDING A POSITION

Imagine different positions that you could take on the following topics:

1. Discuss the comparative strengths and limitations of solar and nuclear energy in terms of cost and environmental safety.

2. Discuss attitudes toward spanking in Canada over the past fifty years. Should spanking remain legal?

EXERCISE SEVEN: BRAINSTORMING
Spend five minutes jotting down everything that comes to mind on the following topics. Then cull the list and group related ideas.

1. Differences in the capabilities of men and women in professional sports result entirely from unequal training. Discuss.

2. "The twentieth century saw poetry decline in popularity while the short story became a more preferred literary genre." Is this true? Why? Why not?

The Thesis

Generating a Thesis

Once you have focused a topic by narrowing it sufficiently and analyzing its component parts, you will be ready to begin looking for a thesis. If the topic can be thought of as the area to be explored, the thesis is the purpose you aim to fulfill when you reach your destination. Every academic essay must have such a purpose: not necessarily an argument *as such*, but a central insight or proposition or explication that captures what you consider to be the most important results of your thinking.

Does every essay, then, have a thesis?

Yes. But it is not always an explicit and identifiable statement. Sometimes the thesis is the general controlling idea that provides overall unity and direction to your essay. Therefore, every essay has a thesis even though not every essay has a thesis statement.

In some disciplines a description may be required in a paper; the students will be asked to do some research, read journal articles or scholarly books, and restate, in their own words, the themes and concepts covered by the authors of these secondary materials. On other occasions they may be asked to do a précis, an abstract, or a prose summary of experimental data. These forms of writing still need to follow formal principles of organization and are still a mirror of the thought processes of the writer. And, even though the writer is not confronted with the mystery of a completely new writing task, even though the introduction, body, and conclusion of the piece are all known at the outset, the organization and presentation are still an expression of personality and mind. One might sit down to describe the mechanics of a hydraulic lock, or the culture of the Mohawks, or the anatomy of a praying mantis, and in each instance there is little or no room for original insights; the research calls only for the retrieval of well-documented facts from the library. Yet in organizing that material, and in rendering it into prose, the choice of word and phrase and the decision of where to begin and end will all be acts of personal imagination and intellect. All this is just a complex way of saying that no integrated body of writing can exist (that is, communicate with its reader) unless it expresses the self-conscious designs of its author. An essay may not require a thesis statement, but it does need to have a principle of organization, some generative and cohesive force to shape, form, and interconnect its sentences. If we define a "thesis" as the sustained purpose, the *raison d'être* of the writing task, then we would say, "Yes, every essay has a thesis because every essay contains the self-conscious purpose of its writer at every stage of its creation."

Whatever your discipline, the thesis is your way into a topic. A topic alone cannot lead you into any kind of academic essay. A topic is merely the terrain you need to keep in view: it is neutral, flat, without intellectual value until an inquiring mind has established a purpose for exploring it. Again, consider the original meaning of the two words, both from classical Greek:

> topic = *topos*, "place"
> thesis = "something set down"

A thesis is something declared, a decision made, a direction found. In its ideal formulation, it is the essayist's crystal-clear apprehension of purpose that acts as gravitational centre and navigational device throughout the course of writing the essay.

At this stage of thinking through your essay, it might be helpful to visualize the process as a series of loosely formed circles. Each circle evolves from the whole; each forms a relationship with the other:

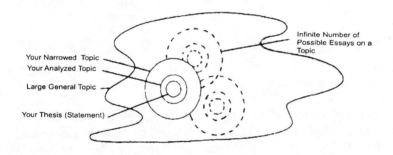

In the following examples, the topic outlines the subject to be covered, and the thesis declares the position the writer has taken.

Examples:

Topic:	The Vietnam War
Narrowed Topic:	American involvement in the Vietnam War.
Analyzed Topic:	What was the most important cause of America's increased involvement in the Vietnam War during the 1960s?
Thesis:	The escalation of the Vietnam War during the 1960s was caused primarily by America's anti-Communist foreign policy.

Topic:	Virginia Woolf's *To The Lighthouse*.
Narrowed Topic:	The last chapter of *To The Lighthouse*.
Analyzed Topic:	What are the major themes? How are these developed? By imagery, especially in the last chapter.
Thesis:	The major themes of *To The Lighthouse* are resolved in the imagery of its last chapter.

Searching for a Thesis

While you are unlikely to know your exact thesis until you have done more reading and possibly begun writing, you should try to approximate it as soon as you can. The process of essay writing is very much a matter of probing ahead at each stage, whether trying to picture the shape of the essay or anticipating what conclusions your investigations are pointing toward. From the earliest stages of the experience, you should be trying to see farther than you can see clearly. When a vivid idea occurs to you (it might be at first only a hunch), follow it through. See how much sense it makes of the topic you are exploring. You might be completely wrong at first; you might go through a dozen formulations over the course of your research period; you might find a bird when you expected to find an aardvark, and then discover that the bird is a sandpiper standing up close when through the fog you thought it was an ostrich a hundred metres away. But if you had not looked for something in particular, you would not have found anything at all. You are much more likely to locate that powerful controlling idea that accurately centres on what you are discovering if you are always looking for it than if you are not. In the course of careful, attentive, and always-ready-to-be-fooled prediction, we probe toward, and ultimately see, exactly what is there.

It is a big mistake to defer thinking deeply about your thesis until all your research is done. Research in this sense is really *search*, a search to find relevant material and make connections. Finding a thesis is a process that begins the moment we embark on a new course of study. Blinding and sudden revelations do occur in academic work, but they are not to be counted on. If you jump into your research and allow yourself to go off in all directions without any idea of what your thesis might be, you increase the chances of wasting time reading material that turns out to be irrelevant. Worse, you could so confuse yourself with undirected information that any possibility of a central organizing idea emerging from the chaos is lost. It is in such cauldrons of conscientiously achieved disarray that the more peculiar and painfully awkward essays are brewed. "All hope abandon, ye who enter here."[2]

The question remains, how exactly do I find this central idea that will bring everything together? It makes sense to begin by thinking about the topic. For example, if you are asked whether the debate about the morality of slavery or economic conditions contributed more significantly to the American Civil War, your thesis will present your opinion of the primary causes of the war and an indication of the reasons for your belief. No doubt you will want to define the various causes as contributing, necessary, or sufficient. Give yourself time to mull over ideas and to imagine how things fit together. Above all, as you generate your thesis, pay attention to any particular aspect of your material that seems of paramount interest and importance to you. You will have little trouble identifying your thesis once you locate a compelling focus.

You will want to decide what kind of essay best suits your subject and your assignment. Will it be necessary to persuade your reader about a controversial point? Do you want to describe something by supplying substantial and convincing data? Or is your purpose to explain something by weighing several different points of view? As you come closer to the point you want to make, the method by which you will be communicating it to your reader will form.

---

[2] Dante Alighieri, "Inferno," *The Divine Comedy*, III.ix, quoted in *Dictionary of Quotations*, ed. Bergen Evans (New York: Avenel, 1978) 165.

Asking Questions to Find the Thesis

If you have done some reading and are still having trouble finding a thesis, try asking the following questions about your material:

1. *Why?*

   Does your material lend itself to answering a "why" question? Why did the event take place? Why were these conditions present? For example, you might explain why Japanese Canadians were so harshly treated during World War II.

2. *How?*

   Could your material provide an answer to a "how" question? Could you explain how a particular cultural practice evolved, or how a bee communicates with other members of its hive, or how decisions are made in the White House?

3. *What?*

   Can you ask what role an historical or fictional figure played in events, what the most important aspect of a theory is, what the function of a specific image is in the work of literature you are studying? For example, you might ask what Lester Pearson's most important contribution to foreign affairs was, or what the green light symbolizes in F. Scott Fitzgerald's novel *The Great Gatsby*. Only be careful that your "what" questions are not simplistic. A university essay should not catalogue historical events or summarize the plot of a novel, which a question like "What happened?" would invite you to do. Your "what" questions should lead you to explain, interpret, or define: not "What people watch television evangelists?" but "What accounts for the popularity of television evangelists?" Useful "what" questions can normally be rephrased into "why" or "how" questions.

Get into the habit of asking all kinds of questions when you are looking for a way into your material. By posing and answering significant questions, you should be able to identify an important and interesting thesis. These general questions — why, how, what, and what if — might lead you to more specific inquiries about your material. Listed below are some approaches you might try:

1. *Cause*

   Are the causes of an event or a process of particular importance? You might look at the causes of an historical event, a sociological phenomenon, or a particular disease. Are the causes contributing, necessary, or sufficient?

2. *Effect*

In looking at your material, can you ascertain important effects or results? For example, what has been the effect of the introduction of oral rehydration therapy in developing countries? Has the use of the Internet contributed to the current North American obesity epidemic?

3. *Comparison*

Does a comparison of certain aspects of your material interest you? Could you compare two theories of chivalry, the humorous techniques of Leacock and Twain, or two sources of electrical power?

4. *Strengths and Weaknesses*

Can you examine the strengths and weaknesses of a theory, a politician, a play? For example, you might consider the strengths and weaknesses of the political policies of prime minister Jean Chrétien, or of Margaret Atwood's argument that the central theme of Canadian literature is survival.

5. *Pros and Cons*

Does your material lend itself to an examination of pros and cons? For example, what are the pros and cons of legalizing same-sex marriage or of chemical and organic fertilizers?

6. *Chronological Development*

Can you trace a development in your material? You might look at the development of a character in a novel, a symbol throughout a poet's works, the evolution of primates, or the transition of a dictatorship to a democracy. Chronology (the development through time) of your material could be its most interesting aspect. For instance, you might argue that Coleridge's awareness of the unconscious and its relation to creativity predated that of both Freud and Jung. Be careful, however. A chronological approach can easily degenerate into a mere recitation of facts and dates with no relevant interpretation of material. Skillfully handled, though, the approach can be interesting, especially when significant connections are made.

Remember that a good thesis:
a) answers the question or fulfills the assignment set by the instructor, and

b) presents the argument that seems most significant and most interesting to you.

The Thesis Statement

Through the process of critical inquiry and research, the writer moves in the direction of transforming topics into theses and in most cases into thesis statements. A strong thesis statement or a strong sense of purpose can make the difference between a rambling essay that seems to circle around the point without ever finding it and an essay with a lively forward impetus that proceeds with deliberate purpose. A carefully chosen thesis statement can prevent both befuddled wandering and mechanical, superficial development. It can do all this, of course, only if you make proper use of it. Even if your thesis does not take the form of a statement, your writing should, with every sentence, convey a sense of purpose to the reader.

You should keep this sense of purpose in mind while you are preparing your outline, doing your research, writing your essay, riding the bus. If it is in the form of a statement, it serves both as centre of gravity and homing device. A clear and succinct statement of your central idea helps you to notice subtle aspects of your topic that support or undermine your purpose. As you toil through a particularly difficult passage, remaining aware of your thesis statement will help you to remain true to the general direction you have set for your paper.

In order to work this way, the thesis must be just right. The purpose you have in mind should be formed sufficiently to be completely integrated with the topic you have chosen. A thesis statement must be short enough (probably one sentence) that you can keep the entire statement in mind as a single object of contemplation. It cannot serve as a useful compass if it points in more than one direction. To get the thesis to a useful stage, you may well have to go through many formulations of it over the course of your preparation for the essay. You may finally find it only by beginning the essay, and once you have written your way into realizing what your thesis is, by starting your paper again. But a good thesis statement is worth the effort. Do not mistake a feeling of familiarity with the subject for an awareness of purpose. Sometimes thoughts must be put to the test of words, submitted to the constraints of strict sentence structure, before we can see illogicalities and foggy patches. It is, after all, the grand claim, distinction, and hope of the university that with careful thinking we can know things more deeply, in greater complexity, and therefore more accurately than without.

Writing the Thesis Statement

The thesis statement, then, declares the controlling idea of the essay: it states the purpose of the essay and indicates the design by which that purpose will be fulfilled. The thesis statement should be a proposition, not a question or a topic. Remember, it is something set down, an assertion or position statement. Because it is a rather large something, it cannot be an isolated detail of the larger question; it must be sufficient and general enough to cover the topic. Consider, for example, the difference between the following topic, question arising from the topic, and thesis statement:

Topic:	Diefenbaker and the Cuban missile crisis.
Question:	What were the results of Diefenbaker's response to the Cuban missile crisis?
Thesis Statement:	Diefenbaker's indecisiveness during the Cuban missile crisis not only damaged his chances of re-election, but also hurt Canada's image abroad.

In this example, the topic is focused on a general area of study, the question indicates the critical point the writer has selected, and the thesis declares the argument the writer will develop. The specifics — incidents of Diefenbaker's indecisiveness, the ways in which these affected his chances of re-election, and Canada's image abroad — will become the material to be covered within the essay.

Thesis statements do not need to be controversial: you may often write a thesis statement with which anyone conversant with the subject would agree. And originality, in the sense of an approach never before committed to paper in the history of academia, is not required before the Ph.D. dissertation. However, good thesis statements are never self-evidently true. Rather, they need the support of the evidence, details, and examples that a thorough consideration of the subject reveals.

The thesis statement may appear in the introduction to your essay or in the conclusion. Often the introduction is the more useful place for it; a statement of your central proposition at the beginning of your essay will enable your reader to see the direction in which the essay is moving. Besides, essays are not mystery novels, and unless you are a master of the technique, you are likely to irritate and confuse your reader by tucking the thesis in the middle of your essay or withholding it until the end. In any case, remember that while the thesis statement is helpful to your reader, its primary purpose in life is to help *you*. No matter where it makes its first appearance in your essay, it should at all times be in your mind.

Complex Thesis Statements
Interesting, well-conceived thesis statements often declare an apparent contradiction. Such theses can be productive of complex, penetrating insights into your material. There are several reasons for this.

First, by its very nature the process of exploring a contradiction requires you to notice the similarities and differences between things, and often we can see something best by defining it not only in terms of what it is but in terms of what it is not.

Second, academic work is aimed above all at discovering the actual nature of things, whether the precise movements of a poem, or the internal chemistry of the DNA molecule, or the specific psychological impulses behind the consumer's choice of a brand-name item. And the actual nature of things, we keep discovering, is complex and contradictory: people can behave like monsters or saints and still be human beings, for example. The compelling quality of much of the world's most powerful literature derives in part from its exploration of some deep contradiction or paradox or irony or tension between opposing forces at the heart of human life. Greek tragedy and English Romantic poetry are two examples, the former obsessed with the gulf between intention and result, the latter with the tension between our constitutional tendency toward apathy and our constitutional capacity for joy.

The complex thesis statement is preferable to the simple one, then, for at least two reasons: it challenges you to analyze your subject more precisely, and it is often a better reflection of the reality of things. In any case, it is disastrous to pretend that something complex can be made simple by loading all the evidence on one side.

A good thesis statement, remember, can propel you through your essay, but only if it declares a sufficiently energetic idea. A statement that holds two contradictory elements in tension usually has the required energy. The tension might be in a contrast between your own and the traditional interpretation of an historical event or literary work, between appearance or reputation and reality, and so on. If you are having trouble finding a thesis, try formulating one that begins with "although." If you set yourself a challenging task at the thesis stage, you will find that you have done yourself a favour when you come to write the essay.

Checklist: Thesis Statements

1. **Does your thesis statement do more than restate the topic or question?** It should present the results of your investigation, not announce your intention to investigate. This thesis statement declares an intention:

   This essay will examine the effects of gamma-rays on man-in-the-moon marigolds.

   This preferred thesis statement indicates the results of a study:

   Gamma-rays cause strange mutations of man-in-the-moon marigolds.

2. **Does your thesis statement reflect the restrictions that your essay will impose on the subject?** For example, this thesis statement does not tell the reader the limits imposed on the main point to be discussed:

   Work exploits people instead of freeing them.

   This preferred thesis statement defines the restrictions:

   The prosperity of investors in twentieth-century Britain depended on the maintenance of a large pool of labour willing to work for minimum wage.

3. **Is your thesis statement written clearly, so that it states the central idea of your essay precisely?** This thesis statement is imprecise and unclear:

   It is hard to say what ever became of Quebec's spirit; the issue has remained unresolved after years of debate.

   This preferred statement indicates the writer's argument:

   Quebec nationalism is not dead; it is merely dormant.

4. Is your thesis statement brief, written preferably in one and no more than two sentences?

5. Does your thesis statement present a proposition that can be supported with evidence? Avoid statements that are narrowly factual, overly subjective, illogical or sensational. Consider this statement:

> Einstein was the greatest physicist of all time. All of his theories were, and continue to be, foolproof.

This is too much to be proven in a single essay. It would be better to evaluate carefully one of his theories, stressing its merits and indicating how it has stood the test of time.

6. **So what?** If you ask this of your thesis statement and nothing comes to mind, your thesis statement reveals nothing of significance, or its truth is too readily apparent. You want your reader to be intellectually responsive to the material you cover and the meaning you create.

EXERCISE EIGHT: FROM TOPIC TO THESIS STATEMENT
Propose a thesis for each of the several hypothetical topics listed below. Do not be too concerned about whether the statement made is right or wrong, accurate or ill-informed. The important thing for the purpose of this exercise is to make a clear, strong statement of your position on the topic. Be creative!

1. The role of the narrator in *Heart of Darkness*.

2. Assess the impact of computers, the Internet, and computer games on an individual growing up in the electronic age.

3. Is state censorship justifiable in the case of hate propaganda and violent pornography?

4. The relations between francophone and anglophone Canadians at the beginning of the twenty-first century.

5. Should the principal purpose of environmentalists be to correct the problems technology creates? Should environmentalists be proactive as well as reactive? If they are proactive, are they not seeking to dominate and control nature in much the same manner as industrial technology does?

EXERCISE NINE: SAMPLE THESIS STATEMENTS

Indicate whether each thesis statement below is good or poor. In the case of a poor thesis statement, indicate by number which of the criteria on the thesis-statement checklist it fails to meet. If you have time, explain your evaluation and propose a better version.

1. This essay will examine the effects of prohibiting fishing in the Otonabee River during spawning season.

2. The development of steel was very important in the growth of a distinctively new architecture both in Europe and in North America.

3. Every socioeconomic group in North America has suffered adverse effects from the growth of technology over the past century and a half.

4. Both in terms of major energy production, such as the generation of electricity for cities, and in terms of localized energy needs, such as the fuel for a single automobile, hydrogen is the power source of the future.

5. Shakespeare's *King Lear* is pervaded by images of animals, of torture, and of clothing.

6. When Prime Minister Pierre Trudeau reluctantly invoked the War Measures Act in October 1970, he was courageously defending his citizens from the imminent loss of their freedoms at the hands of the lunatic fringe.

7. Food processing is not detrimental to the value of the food itself. When we look at nature we see that nuts and seeds are preserved to last over several winters, and honey is really refined sugar.

8. Like many animals, bees can communicate with one another. Bees that have found nectar will return to the hive. There they perform dance-like motions. These motions can communicate information about direction and distance.

9. Although Canada's anti-Jewish immigration policy during the Holocaust has been blamed on the prejudice of a few officials, the main reason for its adoption can be found in Mackenzie King's sensitivity to the political climate of his country: anti- Semitism was a vote-getter.

10. Although Marx debunked religion as "the opiate of the people," the structure of his thought is deeply theological.

11. Life and death are exchanges, not ends.

12. It is no longer the case that the city wastes and the farm conserves: agricultural pollution is posing a considerable threat to the environment. With a diminishing amount of land on which to farm and with heavier use of that land, agribusinesses are facing an ecological crisis.

13. Philosopher John Locke's influence on modern views of liberty is profound.

14. Although one is a high-spirited comedy and the other a brutal tragedy, the medieval plays "The Nativity" and "The Crucifixion" explore a common theme: the intersection of the human and the divine.

15. The younger generation is more aware of the need to protect the environment and trim its lifestyle than the older.

16. Darwin's Theory of Evolution was met with a storm of controversy, with people saying it violated religious beliefs. Why?

17. The prison in the novel demonstrates how its characters are caged mentally and live frustrated lives.

EXERCISE TEN: REFORMULATING THE THESIS
Carefully read the introduction to Sample Essay C in Appendix D and identify the thesis. Now read the essay with that thesis in mind. As you read, try reformulating the thesis so that it more strongly expresses the central proposition of the essay.

3 Research

ALTHOUGH NOT ALL essays are research essays, all essays require research. Research begins as soon as you consult someone or something outside of yourself, and it usually goes on until you have written and revised the last word of your essay. Even if you consult only one external source, a work of literature for example, you are still researching.

Research can be defined as a close searching, a studious, critical investigation of a well-defined topic. The word is derived from the Latin word *circare*, which means "to go round." This is essentially what you do when you research a topic: you try to encircle it, to mark its boundaries. You progress to the subject's core in an ever-tightening spiral. Research helps you to focus your topic, formulate and refine your thesis, and discover details, opinions, and facts against which you can test this thesis.

Because most people are curious, research can become a monster of voracious appetite; it can swell so large that, unbridled, it will eat up all your time and will attempt to eat New York even though your essay topic is Fifth Avenue. You therefore need to take control of the research process from the beginning. Your interests and the demands of your topic and thesis direct your research; the time you have to prepare an essay and its projected length limit it. By following the steps outlined in this chapter, you will be able to control your hunger for tasty but irrelevant details while ensuring that you gather enough substantial information to flesh out your essay.

Primary and Secondary Sources

It is useful to be able to distinguish between primary and secondary sources when researching. Primary sources are original, first-hand materials. Secondary sources are articles, editorials, textbooks, books, and other published materials that interpret the texts, works of literature, data, ideas, events, and so on that constitute primary sources. For example, for an essay on Sir Walter Scott's poetry, the primary sources are the poems; the secondary sources might be biographies of Scott or literary criticism of his work. For a descriptive essay on acid rain, primary sources would be government documents and scientific reports; secondary sources would include journal articles and texts that interpret the facts found in these documents. Sometimes you will be asked to focus entirely on or to use only primary sources in your essay. In that case, the analysis and interpretation of the primary sources will come from you, rather than from other experts.

Preliminary Research

You may need to do preliminary research to find a topic or to refine one. Begin by doing some general reading. There are several good starting places: course syllabi, the required and recommended readings listed in course outlines, textbooks and lecture notes, books and articles dealing with the major themes of your courses. Also useful are the various reference books available in most libraries or on the Internet. Encyclopedias, biographical dictionaries, chronologies, and handbooks can give you an overview of a particular discipline, subject, or era. They can also give you a sense of the range of possible topics open to you, and a sense of the larger context of any one topic that you might have chosen.

Encyclopedia articles are particularly useful in preliminary research, even though any professor would be quite rightly horrified to receive a paper for which such an article constituted the main research effort. Most of us know about general encyclopedias, such as the *Encyclopedia Americana* or the *New Encyclopaedia Britannica*, but there are many specialized encyclopedias that provide detailed coverage of various academic subjects. These encyclopedias are full of articles by scholars who are expert in the fields for which they write entries. Some of these specialized encyclopedias include the *Encyclopedia of Philosophy*, *The International Encyclopedia of the Social Sciences*, and the *McGraw-Hill Encyclopedia of Science and Technology*.

If your topic is a person, an article in a biographical dictionary could fulfill the same purpose as an article in a specialized encyclopedia. These dictionaries generally classify famous people by nationality, historical period, or profession. You can find information on scientists in the

Dictionary of Scientific Biography, and articles on famous governors of Canada, for example, in the *Dictionary of National Biography* (which provides entries on British persons now deceased) and in the *Dictionary of Canadian Biography*. There is even an index to biographical entries in reference works entitled the *Biography and Genealogy Master Index*.

To discover what reference works are available, consult your library's catalogue or web site (which will likely provide a wealth of information designed to help you do your research as easily as possible). Remember, while more and more reference works are becoming available electronically, it is still worth your while to familiarize yourself with the reference book section of your library. Do not hesitate to seek the assistance of reference librarians. They are there to assist you in your research.

Choosing Your Research Direction

Once you have decided upon a topic, analyzed this topic, narrowed it appropriately, defined your special approach to it, and formulated a tentative thesis, you still have at least two decisions to make before your major research effort starts: you must decide how much of the topic needs research, and what kind of research is needed.

Some questions cannot be solved by research alone. A moral or logical problem, for example, might not lend itself to research. Consider the following question:

Is fetal stem-cell research ethical?

Your answer to this would depend more upon your beliefs and upon your capacity to justify these beliefs logically than upon your ability to collect and interpret information. Consider the following essay topic, also about fetal stem-cell research:

Examine the arguments of both the proponents and adversaries of fetal stem-cell research. Is fetal stem-cell therapy an important medical breakthrough, and, if it is, do its benefits outweigh the ethical problems?

In contrast to the first topic, this one requires extensive research.

Once you have determined that your topic requires research, you should think about what kind of research is necessary. What type of information do you need? Can the questions generated by your topic be answered through observation or experimentation? An essay on cadmium uptake in mussels might require both a review of literature on this subject and extensive field work. Perhaps you need to survey opinion or to design and distribute a questionnaire to test the validity of your thesis. Activities such as these require you to generate your own statistical or experimental data. Also, you should be aware that other useful non-print information might be available. You could interview local lawyers and social workers while researching an essay on child abuse in your area, or you might consult a student from Africa before writing an essay on developing countries. Semi-public documents, such as organization and corporate records, might help you when engaged in market research. Trips to various art galleries might be helpful when writing about Tom Thomson's brush technique.

Today, much information that was once available only to those visiting libraries is accessible through the Internet, which allows researchers to read electronic journals, encyclopedias, and dictionaries, as well as to consult library catalogues and databases of statistics or bibliographic entries. This does not mean that library research is not valuable; rather, it means that our definition of the library and of library research has changed. The library is no longer simply a building or the collection housed within a building. Still, many of the questions generated by a topic can be answered only after consulting the documents, manuscripts, audio-visual material, statistics, maps, periodicals, books, and electronic information made available by libraries, museums, archives, and other information centres or services.

Checklist: Choosing Your Research Direction

1. **Can this topic be researched? Can your thesis be supported by discovering facts and how they have been interpreted?** Is your topic too autobiographical or too subjective to demand research? Logic problems or questions based on moral assumptions generally cannot be answered by collecting information.

2. **Is this topic too restricted, too current, or too broad to be researched effectively?** Sometimes, if a topic is very recent or extremely restrictive, there is not enough information available upon which to base an essay. For example, it might be difficult to assess whether the US invasion of Iraq was successful if you

were writing in 2003. Alternatively, a very broad topic must be limited by considering the amount of time you have to research and write the essay, as well as by your essay's projected length.

3. **Is this topic interesting enough for you to spend time researching it?** If you have a choice, try to select topics that seem significant to you. After all, if you are curious about a topic, you will be more likely to spend time researching it, and your research will likely be more directed.

4. **What kind of research is suggested by your topic and thesis?** Imagine that you are researching the status of women in nineteenth-century Canada. Inherent in this subject are as many different research strategies as there are theses. For example, you might choose to examine what the laws of marriage, divorce, property ownership, and the family were by looking at Canada's statutes. You could try to discover how many women worked outside the home and how women's wages compared to men's by investigating statistical sources of information. You could look at women's diaries of the period to see what various women thought their role and status should be, or determine what status men generally ascribed to women by reading literature written by men. Obviously, there are many other directions your research could take. Whatever your topic, the choice of direction is yours.

5. **How available and how complex is the material that must be consulted?** There is no use deciding to write an essay on how children were portrayed in magazine advertisements of the 1950s if you cannot gain access to the appropriate magazines. Also, a student attempting to define and contrast various philosophical and scientific theories of time might find this task too time-consuming because of its complexity.

EXERCISE ONE: CHOOSING YOUR RESEARCH DIRECTION
Use the checklist above to help you think about the following topics.
Which topics demand research, and what kind of research might be needed?
How should this research be limited, and what problems might the
researcher encounter?

1. Describe the occupational hazards faced by workers in nuclear
    generating stations and assess the nuclear power industry's safety
    regulations.

2. Michelet, Marx, and Macaulay were all products of eras of rapid and
    revolutionary change. Examine how their backgrounds influenced their
    concepts of history.

3. Has the creation of a welfare state in Canada led to a significant
    redistribution of income and wealth? Why or why not?

4. Examine how popular music both reflects and influences its audience.

5. Should governments be able to prohibit smoking in public places?

6. Alistair MacLeod reveals a certain ambivalence toward the family in
    his book of short stories *The Lost Salt Gift of Blood*. Discuss the
    significance of the title of MacLeod's book in relation to his portrayal
    of the family.

Library Research

As soon as possible, take the time to acquaint yourself with the organization
of the library. You will find libraries inviting and comfortable once you
know how they are arranged. In fact, most libraries are a little like local
pubs or coffee houses; they attract regulars who come to chat, read, and
dry their socks on radiators. If your library offers tours, whether on site or
online, take one. Are there separate sections for specialized material such
as government documents, maps, rare books, archival material, audio-
visual resources, periodicals, and reference books? Learn how to use the
library catalogue.

Next, browse through the reference section for each subject you take.
All subjects have specialized reference books that you should be aware
of; many of these are available online, but not all. There are too many
different kinds of reference works to mention here. However, besides the
dictionaries and encyclopedias already discussed, there are concordances,
almanacs, chronologies, statistical abstracts, atlases, indexes, abstracts,
and bibliographies.

Often, in the course of essay writing, you will want to retrieve a specific piece of information, a detail to support a point or to close an argument. For example, you might want to know what the chemical composition of aspirin is or how many Canadian military personnel died in World War I. A familiarity with the reference works in your field will allow you to answer these and similar questions quickly.

Most often, however, you use reference works to produce a "working bibliography" of library material potentially useful to your chosen topic. You must make a broad examination of available and relevant books, articles, and other resources before evaluating them in order to determine which will be the most useful to your essay. Sometimes the instructor will provide a preliminary bibliography of suggested or required readings. In this case, it is your job to assess the list, tailor it to your particular purpose, and add to it. Your working bibliography should contain more works than you expect to use because not all of the material will be useful. To develop your list, use the bibliographies, abstracts, and indexes available in the reference section or online, and of course, use the library's catalogue.

Library Catalogues

Most library catalogues are now online and are often only a part of a larger library web site. All catalogues attempt to organize material logically so that it can be found quickly. You can search the online catalogue by author, title, subject, or keyword to find out what is available in that particular library from its collection of books, journals, maps, government documents, videos, cassettes, etc.

Periodicals are usually listed in library catalogues by their complete title and by their general subject only. In other words, the authors and titles of articles published within these periodicals are not listed; you must consult an index for that information.

Author or title searches

If your course bibliography supplies you with authors' names and/or titles of books on your topic, you can use the quick title or author search. Search by a title if you have it, rather than by author; most online catalogues make it easy to search or browse for titles beginning with the words you type in (ignore articles such as "a" or "the"). The first three or four words of a title are often enough to produce what you are looking for. You can also search for journal (also known as "periodical") titles to see if the library carries a journal you need.

When performing an author search, type the last name first and then the first initial. From the list of names that pops up, you can choose the correct one; clicking on it will produce a list of all items by that author in the library. For both author and title search, you can also tell the computer which field(s) to search. You can, for example, limit your search to books if you are not interested in consulting microfiche or dissertations.

Subject and keyword searches

Often when you begin your research, you have only a topic to work with. You then have the option of trying a subject search, or you can search by keyword. Subject searches and keyword searches are different. Subject searches browse the list of *Library of Congress Subject Headings* that are used to classify items in the library's catalogue. Keyword searches browse all items in a database with the words you requested. Keyword searching is effective in any database, the library catalogue, a periodical index, or an internet search engine. When looking for items on a particular topic, the keyword search is easier and more effective than the subject search. To do an effective subject search, you must be familiar with the *Library of Congress Subject Headings*, a guide to which is housed in most academic libraries.

Keyword searches

To perform a keyword search, the researcher asks the computer to look through the database for key words or phrases that describe specific concepts. Sets of concepts are formed and related to one another through the use of keywords and "logical operators" such as "and," "or," and "not."

As an illustration, imagine that you are searching an online catalogue for citations on American responses to terrorism. You would first have to think of all the ways that the concepts "American" and "terrorism" could be represented by keywords. You would then have the tools to create as many different searches as necessary to yield fruitful results.

American	Terrorism
America	Terrorist
United States	Hijacking
U.S.A.	

Focused keyword searches might be

American and terrorism
American and terrorist
American and hijacking
America and terrorism
etc.

Or you could use "or" to indicate that the search should be for items that may have one term or the other, but not both:

American or America or United States or U.S.A.

You could also use "and" and "or" in the same search request, making sure to put brackets around the (or) terms:

(American or America or United States or U.S.A.) and terrorism

There are many other ways to refine keyword searches. Librarians will guide you through the intricacies of developing an appropriate search strategy for your topic.

The Catalogues of Other Libraries

The catalogues of other libraries are available online. Searching these catalogues can aid students in the preparation of working bibliographies. While the material catalogued by these other libraries may not be readily available at your own, it is worthwhile to get a broad overview of what has been published on a particular topic by consulting these catalogues. Also, it is often possible to borrow material from other libraries through your library's inter-library loan system (ILL). Keep in mind that you must place ILL orders ahead of time in order to be sure of meeting your essay deadline. If much of the material you need to consult is available only through ILL, you should begin compiling your working bibliography early in the term. Be sure to get particulars from the inter-library loan office regarding costs or the amount of time needed to fill requests.

Searching for Articles Using Indexes

Articles discovered using indexes can aid your research effort greatly. By using a newspaper index, a history student can find pieces on the abolition of slavery that were published in the *Times* during the early nineteenth century. A student writing an essay on employment equity for disabled persons might be able to demonstrate that media coverage of this topic has increased over the last five years by discovering how many articles on this subject were published in popular magazines during each of the years under consideration.

You will also need to use journals if you must consult the most recent scholarship when preparing your essay. Journals are the regularly published collections of articles — otherwise known as essays — written by researchers currently doing work in their specific fields. A journal article will usually have been written less than a year before the issue in which it is published becomes accessible in the library or online; books, in contrast, can be a few years old by the time they are available. Through journal articles, many researchers and writers give their ideas their first public hearing. Journals thus represent an ongoing conversation among scientists, social scientists, historians, literary critics, and others about current areas of experiment, debate, or discussion. Every university library provides students and researchers with access to thousands of journals, each devoted to a particular area of study (perhaps an area as broad as biology or as narrow as the ecclesiastical history of Sussex), each one published periodically (usually monthly or quarterly) in print, online, or both; at regular intervals, the print journals are bound into a hard-cover volume containing several issues.

As mentioned, library catalogues do not usually contain listings of articles published in journals or other periodicals. Only the periodical's title, authoring body, and general subject heading will appear in most catalogues. Because of this practice, consulting indexes is the key to unlocking a treasure trove of relevant articles in journals, newspapers, and magazines.

Most indexes are now available in electronic form, but a few remain available only in print. The printed ones are usually housed in the reference section of the library and are useful if you wish to locate older articles, i.e., those published more than ten years ago. Indexes, which libraries pay for by subscription, differ from other kinds of databases because they provide material that has been edited prior to being made available through the database. These databases lead you to journal articles and sometimes to other kinds of sources such as Ph.D. dissertations, e-journals, and even books.

Different indexes cover different fields, disciplines, and subjects. Each library will have its own collection, but the following are some that are widely available, to give you an idea of their scope.

EBSCOhost
Academic Search Elite
Canadian Periodical Index
Arts and Humanities Citation Index
JSTOR-The Scholarly Journal Archive
Biological Sciences
Scholar's Portal
MLA (Modern Language Association) International Bibliography

Some of these indexes list only article citations (information on the title, author, journal, and date). Others list citations with abstracts (summaries of the articles). However, many will include the full text of the article, which you can print, save, or e-mail to yourself.

If you are given only the article citation, not the full-text article (and, of course, in a print index that is all that is available), the next step is to find out if your library carries the journal in which the article appears. If you do a title search for the journal on your library catalogue, it will tell you if your library carries it, and if so, in what format and where you can find it in your library. New issues of periodicals are located in a library's current periodicals area, organized alphabetically by title. Older issues are bound and shelved in the regular stacks of the library. Some (such as newspapers) are not bound but are available on microfilm or microfiche, usually kept in special reading rooms. Some newspaper archives are available on CD. Many journals are electronic, only available through the Internet. And, finally, if your library does not have the journal article you need, you may request a copy of the article through inter-library loan or through an online journal article service.

Using indexes to find journal articles takes time, patience, and perseverance. You often need to try several different keyword searches in several different indexes. If you are lucky, you will find full articles online, but, as often, you will need to look and dig. Don't hesitate to ask for help at the beginning; it takes time to get proficient at this skill. Just remember, this is not something you can do efficiently the day before your essay is due.

Other Bibliographies

There are many other bibliographies besides catalogues and indexes that will prove useful to you. Often, bibliographies or lists of works consulted appear at the end of books, articles, and reports. Close attention to the bibliographies and footnotes contained in your recommended readings can help you to develop your own working bibliographies. Also, many times, libraries, librarians, or researchers will compile bibliographies on specific subjects or individuals. Often, university library web sites provide their own bibliographies or subject guides for the different disciplines taught at the institution. These subject guides list the online indexes, print indexes, web sites, e-books, print reference books, and print bibliographies relevant to the subject. These guides are invaluable starting points for research and are particularly useful in pointing you toward academically acceptable web sites for your discipline. Bibliographies are frequently published in book form and distributed to libraries where they are catalogued and shelved in the reference section. There are also more and more online bibliographies. There may be "subject bibliographies" on native education, waste management, European imperialism, or Polynesian art in your library. Bibliographies of the works of well-known authors such as Shakespeare, Melville, Marx, and Rousseau have certainly been compiled. Often these "personal bibliographies" contain not only lists of the writings of these famous individuals, but also lists of the books and articles written about these writings and about their renowned authors.

Finding a bibliography on your particular topic can save you time. Often the compiler will have searched through the appropriate abstracts, indexes, and bibliographies before completing his or her list. If this is so, duplicating this search on your own is unnecessary. However, make sure you evaluate the comprehensiveness of the compiler's search before you decide what research you still must do. Ask yourself what kinds of information have been included in the bibliography. Does it list books, articles, dissertations, government documents, manuscripts, films, or maps? When was the bibliography published? Is the material cited recent enough to be useful? It is wise to estimate the bibliographer's cut-off dates. If the bibliography cites articles published between 1960 and 1990, for example, it may be possible for you to ignore the indexes that list articles published between these two dates. Remember too that bibliographers can be biased. They may have dismissed arbitrarily, or for a particular reason, the works of a scholar or group of scholars.

Bibliographers may also evaluate the information they list. Their evaluations, called annotations, can help you to decide what material to consult closely and what to skim. They might also assist you in determining the order in which information should be studied. Scholars often write annotated bibliographies in conjunction with their scholarship, and such a bibliography is invaluable when you are making research decisions.

Bibliographies can be found by using the word "bibliography" as one of your key words when doing a keyword search of the catalogue. Bibliographies in book form are usually found in the reference collection. Ask your reference librarian about useful bibliographies and where to find them.

Research Strategies

Consulting the references in your sources
If you have already collected some relevant books and articles, look to see what sources the authors of these works used. Maybe some of them would be useful to you. This research strategy is effective because, often, the bibliographies, lists of references, parenthetical citations, and footnotes/endnotes included in scholarly publications alert readers to the most significant primary and secondary literature in the field.

Consulting the references of already found material is particularly appropriate when writing papers for disciplines that value primary sources, such as history. Frequently, a history book or article will provide its reader with a good list of archival material, published diaries, statistical records, judicial and administrative records, parliamentary papers, and contemporary newspapers and journals — primary sources all. A word of caution, however, is necessary. If your topic or your discipline requires that you consult up-to-the-minute research, consulting only the sources of already published works is not for you.

The seed pearl method

Imagine that you have found a gem of a reference, a book or article on your exact topic. Look at how that reference is described in the catalogue, bibliographic tool, or database you are consulting. What subject headings or descriptors have been assigned to it? What significant words appear in its title or abstract? Use this information to search for other treasures. Following are two citations, one from an online university catalogue and the other from a research database. Look at each, and develop a list of other subject headings or terms to search.

Full View From Catalog	record **1** of **1** for search **"UTOPIAN AND SCIENCE FICTION BY WOMEN WORLDS OF DIFFERENCE"** PR 830 .U7 U86 1994 Utopian and science fiction by women : worlds of difference Donawerth, Jane L.	Keep ⌐ **Hold**

Title **Utopian and science fiction by women : worlds of difference / edited by Jane L. Donawerth and Carol A. Kolmerten ; foreword by Susan Gubar.**

Publication info **Syracuse, N.Y. : Syracuse University Press, 1994.**

Physical descrip **xix, 260 p. : ill. ; 23 cm.**

Series Title **(Utopianism and communitarianism)**

Subject term **Feminism and literature.**

Subject term **Science fiction, American--Women authors--History and criticism.**

Subject term **Science fiction, English--Women authors--History and criticism.**

Subject term **Utopias in literature.**

Subject term **Women and literature.**

Added author **Donawerth, Jane L.**

Added author **Kolmerten, Carol A., 1946-**

Call Number	Copies	Material Location
PR 830 .U7 U86 1994	NONE	BOOK Standard shelving location

Title: **Text and pre-text in Le Guin's "The *New Atlantis*".**

Authors: Wymer, Thomas L.

Source: Extrapolation; Fall2003, Vol. 44 Issue 3, p296, 8p

Document Type: Article

Subject Terms: *UTOPIAS in literature
*ALLUSIONS
*FICTION

Reviews & Products: NEW Atlantis (Book)

People: LE Guin, Ursula K.
BACON, Francis
LOVECRAFT, H. P.

Abstract: Comments on the text and pre-texts in the fiction "The *New Atlantis*," by Ursula K. Le Guin. Exploration of the concept of utopia; Failure of the critics to recognize the allusion to Francis Bacon's 1627 book "The *New Atlantis*"; Question of how Bacon's utopia looks like in the context of the future dystopia described by Le Guin; Narrative of the rising island; Allusion to H.P. Lovecraft's story "The Call of Cthulhu".

ISSN: 0014-5483

Accession Number: 11602370

Persistent link to this record: http://search.epnet.com/login.aspx?direct=true&AuthType=cookie,ip,url,uid&db=afh&an=11602370

Database: Academic Search Elite

View Links: get it!
Trent

Notes: Trent Library has this journal - check TOPCAT for holdings. Microfilm V.1(1959) - V.19(1978)

Formats: Citation

© 2004 EBSCO Publishing. Privacy Policy - Terms of Use

Screen capture from EBSCOhost Research Database

Telescoping

One of the most important things to remember when researching is that material on specific subjects often exists within material of a more general nature. You might, for example, find the perfect chapter on economist John Maynard Keynes in a book catalogued only under the subject headings Economists — Biography and Economics — History. If you just search for books about Keynes using his name as a keyword or subject, you will miss this chapter. So remember to vary the scope of your search, especially if the first search strategy you follow does not yield much.

Browsing the stacks

Perhaps it seems old-fashioned, but there's often much to be gained from locating the relevant area of the library and simply browsing for useful information. Online searches don't always yield every possible source, and it is easy to miss a good book or collection of articles turned up by such a search simply because the title fails to grab your attention. As with all research methods, however, don't get carried away by the thrill of being surrounded by books and their attractively musty smell; stay focused, but give yourself time to peruse what's on the library shelves.

Electronic and Online Research

The proliferation of the Internet and the general accessibility of online resources have made traditional library research methods almost obsolete. While this has dramatically increased the availability of research material, it has brought with it numerous potential pitfalls. The rapid changes in the nature and range of online research methods make it impractical for us to outline all of them here. In fact, all good library web sites and online information repositories provide excellent guides to the wealth of data available there.

Instead of providing a guided tour of online resources, in this section we offer a list of the major advantages and disadvantages of conducting research in the booming electronic information marketplace.

Advantages

Accessibility
Most online resources are accessible from any computer connected to the Internet. This allows research to be conducted at any time of the day or night, from almost anywhere, something that is particularly useful for students whose schedules or personal circumstances do not give them the flexibility to work around traditional library hours. Even if the actual consulting of sources must still take place in the library building itself, access to online library catalogues from a remote source enables effective preparation and call-number location to be done in advance.

Quantity of information
The present generation of scholars has immediate access to more information than any of their predecessors. Not only does a standard keyword search yield hundreds or thousands of "hits," i.e., potential sources or sites of pertinent information on the topic, but the Internet also gathers in one (virtual) place a vast range of material that could previously be found only in many disparate locations.

Searchability
Web or database search engines are able to locate web sites, articles, government documents, and other sources quickly and comprehensively. Advanced search options allow the narrowest of searches to take place,

often enabling researchers to locate specific sites or articles that deal with very precise topics. Search engines are not limited to library catalogues, of course: most government, corporate, and institutional web sites have their own search mechanism, and the Internet itself has a range of ever-improving search utilities that scour the entire web in a matter of seconds.

Availability of remote resources

Research in the past was often slower and more time-consuming than it is now because of the need either to travel to another location to consult particular sources or to wait for a book or article to be sent from another institution. While scholars still travel to major libraries or research centres to consult specific sources or collections that are not available online (e.g., rare manuscripts, archival material, personal letters, and diaries), the material needed for most undergraduate papers is readily available somewhere in electronic format; and if it is not, the process for locating it and ultimately obtaining it has been speeded up through advances in online search techniques and co-operative agreements between libraries to share information and provide much easier access to catalogues and online resources housed on institutional web sites.

Access to online journals

A major shift in library acquisitions has been the rapid increase in the number and availability of online scholarly journals. Since journals are the life-blood of academic disciplines, fuelling their scholarly debates and introducing cutting-edge research and thinking, this change has been a positive one. The advantages to libraries are important: online journals typically save money and space and allow a library to enhance its journal holdings quickly and easily. Even more important are the advantages to researchers, since online journals can be searched more efficiently, articles can be printed directly from home or office computers, and journals that would not normally be available in print form, especially in smaller libraries, are now readily accessible online. Online journals have revolutionized research and now allow all students to become familiar with journals early in their university career — something that faculty applaud.

Access to shared information networks

As discussed above, the interconnectedness of online resources has made available to more scholars the material and information previously stored at one institution only. Even when online resources first became common, access was limited; now, with faster telecommunications connections and download times, combined with a general willingness among academic institutions and other organizations to share material, many more resources are just a mouse-click away. There is no doubt that changes in the way information is transmitted instantly around the globe have had a positive influence on the academic world, of which the university essay is a part. But we are always cautioned that technological change brings with it certain hazards. Fewer people now are as reluctant to embrace technology as they were in the past, but almost all university professors are acutely aware of the dangers of an over-reliance on electronic research, particularly web-based research. Let's look at some of those possible pitfalls now.

Disadvantages

Information overload
Sometimes the sheer mass of information and material that even the most basic web search yields can be overwhelming. It's often daunting enough to have to comb through several books on your topic, taking notes and formulating ideas as you go, without also having to cope with dozens (or even hundreds) of additional sources of information appearing on your computer. Sifting through this material requires organization and precision, a meticulous eye for what is relevant and what is tangential, and the self-discipline to stop and proclaim, "No more!"

Online research, in fact, requires more than simply access to a computer and a search engine. You need to consider what is involved in conducting a useful online search, planning your strategy in much the same way as you prepare for traditional research: narrowing your focus as much as possible, establishing what you're looking for and where you're likely to find it, and resisting the temptation to get sidetracked. If your search must be a broad one, do it early enough in the research process that you can afford some browsing. An analogy from the shopping mall might help: if you know precisely what you want to buy, you arrive at the mall, head for the appropriate store, buy your item (perhaps comparing a few along the way), and then leave; there's no time for window-shopping. However, if you're in no rush to buy, you do have the time to browse, gathering as much data as you can on your prospective purchase before you make it, allowing yourself the luxury of being lured into something more interesting along the way. Academic essay writing rarely provides such pressure-free browsing time, however, so *caveat emptor*: buyer (or researcher) beware!

Reliability of information
If any one of us wanted to establish a web site devoted to nuclear fission, the works of Chaucer, the history of China, or any other topic, we could do so — either by ourselves or with some technical assistance. It might look very appealing and contain a wealth of information, and a search engine would probably find it. But how trustworthy is the site? Unlike publishing a scholarly book or journal article, both of which are labour-intensive and

often slow processes subject to intense scrutiny and thorough review by one's peers, online publishing is fast, usually unsupervised, easy, and free. Therein lies the central problem of the reliability of online sources. You must, therefore, evaluate every online source you encounter. Use the checklist below as a guide.

Checklist: Evaluating Electronic Sources

1. **Who is the publisher or host of the web site?** Sites hosted by governments, educational institutions, newspapers, professional organizations, etc., are probably more reliable than those hosted by individuals. Web sites with corporate sponsorship could well be reliable, but you will want to consider the issue of bias in the material.

2. **Who is the author of the site?** If you cannot locate an author for the site or page, question its reliability. If you do find an author, find out as much as you can about his or her background, qualifications, and reasons for publishing on the site. What is the author's reputation?

3. **What is the date of publication?** Some pages can stay on the Internet for years and still be found by search engines. Perhaps the material is dated and therefore no longer relevant, so ensure that you are finding the most current information on your topic.

4. **Is the site or page accurate?** Just because it's published on the Web does not mean it's true. Critically examine the information you find and assess its credibility before blindly using it to support your argument.

5. **Does the site or page include a reference list to support its own claims, or links to other sites?** To enable others to evaluate your use of online resources, be sure to record accurate bibliographic information (particularly a complete and accurate URL) and print all web pages and search results that you use.

Neglecting important resources in traditional formats

Another drawback of relying on online sources of information during the research process is that you could exclude traditional sources of information in print form. The relative comfort of sitting at home conducting research can make visiting the library less attractive (especially in cold weather), so relying simply on information gleaned from online sources is often tempting. Much important material is available only in the library itself: government documents, archive material, maps and photographs, rare books, for example. Looking for information online should be viewed as a method of facilitating research, not as the only medium for obtaining material. Granted, a lot of wonderful resources can be found online that cannot be found (easily or at all) in libraries; but the opposite is true, too. And over-reliance on online sources can make the drawbacks described in this section even more of a risk.

Risk of plagiarism

Many professors lament the advent of the Internet and its proliferation as a research tool for one simple reason: the increase in plagiarism. Plagiarism (discussed on pp. 86-87) is the most serious of all academic offences, and involves passing off the words or ideas of others as one's own. The Internet is a haven for those who wish to plagiarize intentionally since it has a number of sites where essays can be bought for a small fee. Aside from the fact that this is academic dishonesty at its most repulsive, professors are just as proficient as students in using the Web to trace suspected plagiarism.

It is unintentional plagiarism that concerns us more here. Effective essay-preparation strategies — such as those described in the chapters on topic and thesis, notetaking, reading, and prewriting — can be tremendously helpful to you in avoiding plagiarism, since they instill in you good habits that remove the danger of accidental plagiarism. Careless notetaking, and the tendency to cut and paste information quickly and easily from a web site or downloaded article directly into a paper, can be principal reasons for plagiarism, so consider the following factors as you incorporate source material into your essay:

1. **Be sure to indicate clearly what is quoted directly and what you are paraphrasing**. Paraphrase effectively: don't simply substitute synonyms. For example, let's say you find an ideal passage in an article on a web site. You cut and paste it into your word-processing program but don't want to quote it at length. You change a few words but retain the overall structure and logical progression of the argument; being diligent, you add a proper citation in the form of a parenthetical reference or footnote. This may not be as serious

as plagiarism, but it is certainly considered an inappropriate use of sources. You are better to consider what the passage states, reflect on it, take notes on it, and then rewrite it completely in your own words, summarizing where necessary and perhaps combining information from that source with information from other sources.

2. **Don't let the overwhelming amount of information force you to sacrifice your own ideas so that you can include all the support you've found.** Use support judiciously; choose quality of supporting material over quantity.

In short, despite the marvellous possibilities made available by the wealth of online resources, you should not let the relative convenience, speed, and comfort of the new research process translate into a neglect of the good habits you need to establish as an academic essay writer. Technology is no substitute for the thorough and critical investigation that is the hallmark of the essay.

Checklist: Selecting Research Material

1. **Do not choose only general material.** Choose some books or articles that are clearly focused on your subject.

2. **Do not choose only secondary sources of information if your topic requires consulting primary sources.**

3. **Do not choose only books and articles that support one another.** If different perspectives are possible, your essay should try to take into account those that contradict your own as well as those that support it. Abstracts, tables of contents, introductions, and summaries may indicate a writer's perspective.

4. **Choose books that are as up-to-date as the subject demands.** In some fields, such as genetics, research material dates quickly; in other fields, such as English, it does not date in the same way.

5. **Consider the author's reputation.** Check the bibliography or reference list. Has the author taken

major works into account? Is she or he mentioned in other people's works? In what connection? Make sure that the author is scholarly if you are planning to present him or her as an academic authority. It is possible that your essay topic requires you to investigate the opinions of popular writers, scientists, psychologists, philosophers, and historians, but do not misuse their work. Scholars provide evidence to back up assertions and citations to back up evidence; popular writers may not. For this reason, your instructor will tend to view the scholarly writer as the more authoritative. Be particularly cautious of the issue of reputation when using electronic sources.

6. **What press published the book?** Different presses have different priorities. Learn to recognize which publishing houses regularly publish scholarly books. The information in these books may be more reliable and will be better documented than that in books published by the popular press.

7. **What periodical does the article appear in?** Do you know anything about its biases or its reputation? *The New Internationalist* is likely to publish articles of a different perspective than the *Financial Post*, for example.

8. **Do not rely solely on electronic sources unless specifically instructed to do so.** If you do consult online resources, be aware of their advantages and disadvantages.

The process of evaluating a text's significance and usefulness does not end here. As you continue to scrutinize the library material or online resources you have selected as pertinent to your topic and thesis, you must constantly think critically about them. A fuller understanding awaits a closer reading, and it is to reading that we now turn.

4 Reading

ALTHOUGH MOST SECONDARY and post-secondary students know how to read, very few of us spend much time thinking about the act of reading. If questioned, we would probably say that we read in order to discover an author's ideas. In fact, what we learn from reading is not simply what the author intended; we also derive meaning as a result of our interaction with the text. Sometimes the author's intent and our interpretation are one and the same; often, they are markedly different.

That reading involves the interaction of text and reader has important ramifications for the essayist. It suggests, first of all, that in order to learn the most from a text, one must read it actively and critically. The passive reader accepts what the author states and therefore limits comprehension; the active reader can move beyond what the author writes to see its implications. Secondly, that meaning is created in the interaction between text and reader implies that the reader can take control of the text. He or she need not bow to the demands of the unseen author by reading a text in its entirety. In fact, the reader can decide both what to read and how to read it.

In this chapter, we focus on both efficient reading and critical reading, providing strategies that allow the researcher to use texts to maximum advantage. The advice we offer may alter your image of reading as a relaxing and effortless act, but we think you will find the reading process more rewarding as you learn to involve yourself in it.

Any kind of reading, whether critical or efficient or both, requires that you pay attention to what you read. It is possible to go through the motions of reading and fail to comprehend a single word: the eyes go over the words, line by line, page by page; half an hour elapses before you read, "The butler did it." "Did what?" you ask, and only then realize that your eyes may have been moving, but your mind has been wandering. You reread the last twenty pages and find that you have missed a murder, a religious conversion, and an avalanche.

Attending to the task of reading requires that you counteract the natural tendency of the human mind to seek the easiest route. This tendency has been responsible for many fine innovations, perhaps for our survival as a species, but it contributes little to the process of reading. Do not sit back in an armchair, book in one hand and potato chips in the other, hoping to absorb what you need to know. The mind absorbs very little indeed. In fact, the mind is excellent at screening out, dismissing as unimportant, and otherwise shirking the work of remembering and integrating new information and ideas. It has to be: the mind gets tens of thousands of pieces of information every day — sights, sounds, smells, touches, tastes — and dismisses most of them as old hat, or maybe as not appreciably different from old hat. Without this automatic selection process that separates the familiar from the unfamiliar, we would live in an hallucinatory, chaotic state, beset by a constant onslaught of images flooding in through the associative process whenever we think or notice anything. It is good, ultimately, that we screen, but the tendency means that we must work hard to absorb anything in a useful way.

You can force your mind to work harder by taking the following approach when you read. First, review the title and table of contents of the work at hand to get an overview of the material. Then, instead of reading for hours at a time, read for shorter sessions. The length of these should be determined by your purpose. If you want to recall details from your reading, half-hour sessions are best; if you need overall argument, longer sessions may be more appropriate. Stop for five minutes after each session to take notes, to think about what you've read, to try to recall the main points. (The mind's capacity to accommodate new information before it must do something to hold onto it is limited.)

Once you have finished a text, review all of your notes. Try to recover a sense of the overall structure of what you have read. The mind is much better at remembering something new when a) it has done something with it, and b) it can place pieces into a structured whole.

Efficient Reading

Reading actively to promote concentration is important, but the effective essay writer must also develop some skills for reading efficiently. For many students, completing the research for a paper is the most enjoyable part of the essay-writing process. Essays, however, have deadlines, so the temptation to indulge in reading's pleasures must be resisted, at least to some extent. The amount of reading and research you do is determined by the time restrictions placed on you. Consequently, learning to read efficiently is often as necessary a skill as learning to write effectively.

The phrase "efficient reading" might conjure up images of timers and multiple-choice comprehension quizzes, but it should not be confused with speed-reading. To read efficiently is to adjust how you read to what you read. Before you open the book or begin the article, you should be able to say what you need to know from it. It is not always necessary to consider every word; sometimes ten minutes of skimming is sufficient to extract what is relevant in a text. The key to efficient reading is thus flexibility in reading rate: adapt your speed to a consciously defined purpose. Naturally, the more detail you require from your text, the slower your reading pace may be. You should be aware, however, that slower is not always better; skimming and scanning techniques will also be appropriate for certain kinds of material and reading purposes.

Organization and Agenda

For both primary and secondary reading, the first step in reading efficiently involves the selection and organization of reading material. Not all works need a thorough reading; by determining and maintaining a clear purpose while you read, you should be able to avoid collecting that wheelbarrow full of notes which only clutters your desk and mind.

As you worked your way through the library catalogue, indexes, and government documents preparing a working bibliography, you obtained a formidable pile of materials, all of which appear to be valuable and relevant. The temptation is to start at the top of the pile and begin reading. But if you are to maintain control of the reading process, you must have more discipline.

Begin the task of reading by surveying each piece of material you have deemed worthy of retrieval. Look at the title, the table of contents, the introduction, the conclusion. Try to arrive at an understanding of the thesis in each article or book. Then, arrange the texts and other sources in the order in which you intend to consult them, using your thesis as a guide to determine priorities. You have now compiled a reading agenda, a guide that should prevent you from devoting too much time to material only indirectly relevant to your proposed paper.

The rate at which you read the texts selected will vary along a spectrum, depending on the importance of the material perused. At this point, you should determine reading rate for each text. The information from which you derive your own argument, for example, needs to be thoroughly understood, so it demands strategies for *detailed understanding*. After all, you want your ideas to be as water-tight as possible. Chances are, however, that the works that comment upon the initial information will begin by reviewing material with which you are already familiar. For these articles or books you can use your skimming skills to deal with information related to your own ideas but not forming their foundation, information about which you need *general knowledge*.

Once you have separated documents that require detailed study from those that may be skimmed, draw up a schedule that not only lists the readings in order of importance but also includes the amount of time you think necessary for each reading. Be flexible and realistic; don't force yourself to snap the book shut if you exceed the allotted time by ten minutes or even a half hour. The key is to avoid the reading trap — take control of the material before it devours you.

Reading for Detailed Understanding

To acquire a thorough understanding of a text, be aware of your reading process as you go through the work. It is not enough to slow down, for in reading slowly you may lose the thread of the author's argument. Rather, try to read *actively*. You should not allow the words simply to wash over you; neither should you memorize them. Instead, ask questions of the text and try to incorporate the responses into your existing knowledge. Force yourself to think about material from a critical perspective and to interact with it.

Active reading can be facilitated by considering the way an author has constructed the text. Writers have similar goals: all want to present arguments or relay data comprehensibly and persuasively. Hence, an author uses many of the same techniques for written expression that we discuss in this book: thesis, underlying structure, appropriate arrangement of ideas, logical paragraph development. As with other aspects of the essay-writing process, it is greatly to your advantage when reading to understand how everything fits together before focusing on one particular paragraph, then another, and so on. Part of the reading process is architectural: if you try to imagine the structure of the text you are about to read, you will be better able to understand how the pieces fit together while you are reading. This practice improves both memory and comprehension, to say nothing of reading pleasure. Just as the writer keeps the reader in mind, the reader keeps the writer in mind. Your initial questions should be "Who is writing?" and "For what purpose?"

The points of advice that follow will enable you to detect organizational structure and are useful in a close reading of central material. They will lead to as much comprehension as the writer's degree of clarity allows. Because you should look at the whole to understand its parts, the three steps outlined below move from the general to the specific. For detailed understanding, it is probably appropriate to follow the entire sequence.

1. **Survey the work.** Remember, the author wants you to be able to understand the argument made and will have tried to make that argument apparent. A quick glance through the work should permit you to predict the nature of the ideas presented. Here's what to look at:

    a) *The title.* A title such as "Spruce Bud Worm: Much Ado About Nothing" suggests not only the topic, but also the direction of the thesis. The author evidently believes that the aforementioned beast is not a serious threat — a useful piece of information that will help you to forecast the nature of the evidence in the paper.

    b) *Table of contents/subject headings.* A good table of contents is like an outline: it will indicate the shape of the author's argument. What is considered first? Last? Which sections are the largest? What gets short shrift? Knowing this sort of information before you begin reading will make you more alert to an author's biases.

    c) *Introduction.* An author's introduction is just like yours. It should contain a thesis, or establish the terrain to be explored, and state priorities. Sometimes the author will explain how the present work fits into existing scholarship in the field: for instance, the author may distinguish his or her argument from that of other scholars, or indicate to which scholars the piece is indebted for specific ideas. The introduction is often used to justify the book's existence and to explain to the reader how and by whom the book should be read. If it is written well, the introduction will act as a guide for the entire text, rather like an instructor's introductory lecture on a subject.

    d) *Conclusion.* Again, if it is written properly, the conclusion should provide a good sense of the author's argument, where it ends up, and what the author considers most important about the subject.

Surveying the text is essential preparation for the more detailed reading that follows. You now have a context — a place prepared — for the information you will acquire in a more detailed reading.

2. *Determine your purpose.* Reading for research is not reading for pleasure, although it can be pleasurable. You have a specific purpose in reading a text; before you begin to read, determine what that purpose is. For example, if you are writing on an assigned essay topic, review the questions asked by the professor. Compile your own set of questions as well. Knowing what you want to discover will allow you to read more actively, to pay particular attention to the passages most relevant to your purpose, and to skip what is irrelevant. The reader who does not have a purpose in mind quickly sinks into the text, losing stride, or skims it frenetically, gaining nothing of use.

3. *Read for meaning.* As we have said, writing effectively on any topic demands a sound understanding of the material. Dense prose, however, can sometimes seem incomprehensible; lengthy sentences, unfamiliar words, and uncommon diction frequently obscure meaning. Use your knowledge of essay structure and language to decipher difficult passages.

   a) *Check for patterns of rhetorical and organizational development.* Is the author dealing with a subject chronologically? Is there a movement from general to specific ideas? Is there a cause-and-effect development? Pay particular attention to transitional words and phrases, for they can supply a context for the sentence or paragraph to come. You can find more information about methods of development and transitions in the chapters on prewriting and drafting.

   b) *Use paragraph structure to decipher a passage.* Every author knows that a paragraph should contain one main idea. Try to determine what that idea is. If you are lucky, the author will have provided a topic or summary sentence to do this work for you.

c) *Break down the sentences* if the prose is particularly difficult, or if the sentences are extremely complex. Read aloud through difficult passages, concentrate on key phrases, try to parse the sentence. Often, knowing the subject and verb of a thirty-word sentence can unlock its meaning.

d) *Keep a dictionary close at hand* as a matter of course, and use it! In some disciplines, a glossary of terms may be helpful. Look up any words essential to your comprehension and write the relevant definition in a notebook devoted to the purpose. In fact, whenever you read, jot down any words you decide to look up later. Set aside half an hour a week to find and transcribe definitions for them.

Detailed understanding should be your first aim in reading central material, and gaining such comprehension may occupy a good deal of your research time, no matter how effective your reading methods. Do not be dismayed. Keep in mind that you must comprehend as thoroughly as possible the material that forms the basis of your argument. It is to your advantage that your ideas be well founded. The time invested will pay off when you write.

Reading for General Knowledge

Not all material, however, is central. A strategy such as skimming can help you to work quickly through more peripheral material, and most readers skim without realizing it. Skimming is what we do when we flip through *The National Enquirer* in the grocery store looking for the juiciest bits. However, academic journals and books are not usually constructed with inflammatory headlines and tell-tale subheadings, so, once you have separated what is central from what is supplementary, you need to know how to cope with the latter.

A skilled reader skims for two reasons: either to locate a specific piece of information or to grasp the main ideas and a few significant details in a selection. Before you decide to skim, then, determine your purpose, just as you would before you read for detailed understanding. In skimming, however, your purpose should be quite narrow.

If you consult a dictionary for a word, or an encyclopedia or other reference work to find the date of an event, for example, you will skim. Your eye skips down the page until it meets with the relevant word or numbers. Whenever you use this technique, be sure you keep in mind the precise detail for which you are searching. The active mind will naturally want to continue from Napoleon to narcissism. Don't get sidetracked!

More frequently, however, your purpose in essay research calls for skimming that will enable you to get the gist of an argument without noting all its supporting details. You will probably use this technique if your reading agenda indicates that an article might be useful but need not be read thoroughly, or if a book chapter contains nothing new but may be too important to your essay to risk eliminating from your agenda. This could be the case with an article or a book that your instructor has mentioned or one to which your other readings make reference. Skimming for main ideas and important details involves techniques quite different from skimming for a specific fact. Most readers skim through articles or chapters using the following steps:[1]

1. *Skim* the introductory paragraph(s) to establish the author's thesis or locate the thesis statement.

2. *Read* the first sentence or two of each paragraph to give you the main idea of the paragraph. Together, these should show the pattern of thesis development.

3. Let your eyes *scan* the paragraphs noting names, dates, and numbers to fill in one or two details.

4. *Read* the concluding sentence of each paragraph, especially if you do not yet have a fairly clear idea of the paragraph.

5. To remember what you have skimmed, make a brief three- or four-sentence *note* describing the essence of the article and considering how it might be relevant to your essay.

Whether you skim or read for detailed understanding, be sure that you keep your purpose in mind. If you use your thesis to monitor what and how you read, you should be able to make the best use of limited time. Leave passive pleasure reading for post-essay exhaustion or warm summer afternoons at the lake.

---

[1]Books may also be skimmed using this method, but exert some caution. You will need to read the introductory and concluding chapters in their entirety to feel confident in your knowledge of the argument made.

EXERCISE ONE: READING FOR DETAILED UNDERSTANDING
We have described a three-step approach to reading for detailed knowledge: survey the text, determine your purpose, and read for meaning. To test the validity of this method, try the following experiment. Read one chapter of a textbook through from start to finish, without using this method. After you have finished, jot down what you remember of the chapter. Then read another chapter, this time using the three-step approach. Again, jot down what you recall from your reading. Compare the results.

EXERCISE TWO: READING FOR GENERAL KNOWLEDGE
A good deal of information can be gleaned from a text using the surveying method described above: looking at the title, the table of contents, the introduction, and conclusion. To test this out, pull an unfamiliar book from a library shelf. Survey it for fifteen minutes, and then record what you have discovered. What is the central thesis of the text? Is the work a scholarly or popular publication? How could the text be used in an essay?

Critical Reading

Regardless of the nature of your reading material, whether directly related or tangential, you should not accept it as absolute truth. There is room for disagreement in every academic subject: scientists argue with each other through the vehicle of equally factual articles, and certainly much writing done in the humanities can be described as the presentation of particular points of view. As you have probably already discovered, language is a powerful tool; the most feeble argument can sound convincing if masked in eloquent prose. To read effectively, therefore, and certainly to analyze perceptively, the student must be prepared to interact with the text. Try always to assume a skeptical position the moment your eyes rest on a page of print: remind yourself that paper will not refuse ink. Evaluate whatever you read; think of the material from the point of view of its context, its author, and its argument. At the same time, be conscious of your own perspective and bias. To increase your sensitivity to an argument's merit, keep the following points in mind as you read.

Your Own Prejudices

It is too simple, when confronted with an argument contrary to one's own beliefs, to reject it out of hand. To respond thus is particularly inappropriate in essay research, because an instructor expects students to address opinions divergent from their own. The work of Karl Marx cannot be dismissed simply because you have undying faith in the capitalist system. Judge an argument on its own merits; do not allow your biases and preconceptions to interfere with your evaluation. The poet Coleridge, a voracious reader and astute critic, followed this maxim: "Until you understand a writer's ignorance, presume yourself ignorant of his understanding."[2]

The Context of the Work

Where a reading comes from and who it is written for often affect its meaning. For this reason, it is crucial to place any work in context, to consider its origins.

For example, were you writing a paper on eugenics (the belief that only certain segments of society should be allowed to procreate), placing in context the work of authors who support this belief in context would be essential to treating their work fairly and accurately. Francis Galton, who is usually considered the founder of the eugenics movement, sincerely believed that eugenics was necessary for the improvement of mankind.

---

[2]Samuel Taylor Coleridge, *Biographia Literaria*, ed. George Watson (London: J.M. Dent & Sons, 1971) 134.

Today, the consensus in Western society is that any sort of eugenics policy would be completely unacceptable. To understand why Francis Galton believed what he did is to understand the context in which he wrote. Modern attitudes toward eugenics are shaped largely by what we now know about environmental influences, heredity, and the political dangers of a eugenics policy, information that was not available to Francis Galton. Were you writing a paper arguing that controlled procreation should be permitted in some circumstances, using Francis Galton's ideas to defend your thesis would thus be inappropriate, since he was not privy to the same knowledge as you are.

Conversely, were you arguing against eugenics, you would also have to judge Galton within the framework of his historical context. That is, you might still claim that his beliefs were morally wrong, but you would recognize that, were he alive today, he might not have held those beliefs.

Even when you are working primarily with contemporary publications, context can be important. The journal in which an article appears, for example, may affect how you interpret it. Scholars still exist who support eugenics, and their articles are published, albeit in journals whose audience may be very limited. You may use these articles, but read them critically; again, remember that the printed word is not always accurate.

The best means of recognizing context is to read widely on your topic from as many diverse sources as possible. By comparing your readings, you will soon be able to determine the context in which each of them was written.

The Author's Approach

As you know, authors usually write about ideas they believe, and their writing is invariably affected by their beliefs. Look for subtext. Try to determine not only what an author is saying, but also what preconceived notions allow the author to arrive at the stated opinions. In particular, focus on the following:

1. *Intent*
   What does the author hope to achieve? To convince the reader of something? To arouse sympathy? To inspire indignation? If the author is making an argument, what is it? Does it achieve its purpose? Remember, authors use language to further their intent, so if you determine direction, you can better perceive purposeful emphases on some aspects of the topic and polite ignorance of others. You can anticipate, for example, that a writer trying to protest the seal hunt will ignore the facts that chickens and cows suffer fates as grim as do seals and that

some Newfoundland residents depend on the hunt for their livelihood.

2. *Attitude*

How seriously does the author take the material and the readers? A writer for *A Star-Gazer's Guide to the Heavens* may presume the reader to be unquestioning; an astronomer published in the *University of Toronto Quarterly* will expect the reader to be critical.

3. *Tone*

Is it serious, lighthearted, condescending, ironic? Beware of tone, for it can be a persuasive tool. A condescending writer can make the reader feel stupid for not agreeing with the position advanced; a lighthearted writer can be convincing simply by virtue of a pleasant tone.

4. *Bias*

Does the author show any prejudice in the selection and interpretation of evidence? Watch for the issues an author avoids, and the ones dwelled upon. An article discussing major Canadian authors that mentions only anglophones is open to criticism. Bias is, however, usually more subtle; the alert critical reader will watch for it at every turn.

5. *Assumptions*

Assumptions are values or opinions that the writer has already "taken up" into his or her thinking, and on which part of the argument put forth is constructed. They are not addressed directly within the paper in question, although the author might well have thought carefully about the matter beforehand. Often the assumption is connected with a broad philosophical, political, or religious allegiance. For example, authors of some newspaper editorials in the 1960s criticized universities for not taking disciplinary action against faculty and students who participated in anti-Vietnam war demonstrations. One of their assumptions — that the role of universities is to defend rather than challenge the authority of government — was based on a philosophical notion about the nature of democracy.

6. *Implications*
   Are certain judgments and conclusions suggested without being stated directly? These are the ideas "implicit" to an argument: "entangled" in it but never explicitly acknowledged. When a federal official calls for environmental reform, the implication is that government money will have to be spent. Whereas arguments are built on assumptions, arguments include implications.

Strategies for Persuasion

Most writers use a range of strategies to convince their readers. Many of these strategies in themselves are not faults; on the other hand, they do not take the place of convincing evidence and sound argument. Authors convince either by being logical and objective or by sounding logical and objective. Make sure your sources are all that they seem. Remember, if you are not reading critically, an author may affect you more by style than by content.

1. *Use of Language*
   Denotation and Connotation. Writers choose words not only for their literal meanings but also for their acquired meanings and associations. Be careful to distinguish between the denotation and connotation of words. For example, we all know what the words "soda pop" denote. What they connote, however, is the memory of a bygone era, and thus they are often used by writers to evoke nostalgic sentiment.

   Up-labelling and down-labelling. These involve the use of particular words to create favourable or unfavourable responses. "Matchbox" is a down-label for a house of modest size; "cosy home" is an up-label.

   Innuendo and implied statement. This rhetorical strategy could be used to manipulate the reader's response. An example might be, "Of course, considering his past, X would not be as supportive of drunk-driving legislation as most of us would be."

   Figurative language. This strategy can make meaning more vivid, which is fair enough as long as the image accurately reflects the situation it renders. "A tiny cherub weeping softly" figures the literal crying child rather differently than "a howling five-year-old monster." Which phrasing is more figuratively appropriate depends on the actual behaviour of the child or upon the author's purpose in describing the scene.

2. *Use of Authorities*

Do not accept authorities unquestioningly: they may be quoted or paraphrased out of context. Furthermore, since authorities do not always agree with one another, the word of one is not necessarily indisputable. Sometimes authors invoke the sound of authority with expressions such as "Research has proven that . . ." or "History shows that . . . ." Evidence that is introduced in this way may be accurate, but you should be wary of it. The authority of personal experience (and of 2nd, 3rd, or nth hand experience) should also be questioned: is there more solid evidence that supports or disputes this material?

3. *Opinions and Generalizations*

Watch for unsubstantiated opinions and generalizations. Do not be fooled by a writer who masks a weak argument with an apparently methodical and logical approach.

4. *Appeals*

Recognize when the author is appealing to your sense of pity, indignation, or outrage, rather than to reason. A sincere author can be sincerely wrong.

Errors in Reasoning

When an essay topic demands a critical examination of an article or book (in philosophy or historiography, for example), you may wish to give an author's argument even closer scrutiny. The most astute scholar will occasionally employ faulty reasoning to arrive at conclusions, and discovering these errors can permit you to discount an entire thesis.

The ability to perceive reasoning errors is also an essential skill in consumer society. The effectiveness of many advertisements and sales pitches depends upon the failure of the client to detect an illogical argument. Learn to recognize the following errors and you will have a formidable defence against any pedlar of great deals who comes to your doorstep.

1. *Is the author avoiding the question?* Does she or he talk around the problem without coming to grips with it? You probably do this yourself. When confronted by an instructor who demands an explanation for a late paper, you may supply a list of all the great

ideas you have for a thesis, without adding that the paper is late because you spent the weekend at a concert or a rowing regatta.

2. *Is the author begging the question?* Is the evidence the same as the conclusion; or, in order to accept the evidence, must you already accept the conclusion? An example of begging the question would be a politician saying, in reference to Arctic sovereignty, "American oil tankers have a perfect right to travel through international waters." The debate in this issue is about whether those waters are international; the politician's assertion demands the reader to accept that they are.

3. *Is the author saying that something is true simply because there is no evidence to show that it is false?* This argument is a common, if illogical, defence for the existence of an omnipotent being; it can't be proven that God doesn't exist.

4. *Is the author failing to apply his or her reasoning and standards of judgment consistently?* Parents, for example, might condone teenage sex in principle, but condemn it when practised by their own children. This error is known as special pleading.

5. *Is the author attempting to discredit an argument by bringing irrelevant, often personal, considerations against the other party?* "The people behind this project are wild-eyed environmentalists" is irrelevant to any essay that evaluates proposals to limit industrial emissions.

6. *Is the author indulging only in black-and-white thinking?* Does he or she think only in terms of extremes while ignoring the possibilities in between? Issues rarely divide themselves neatly into polar opposites; any author who endeavours to make this sort of division should be suspect. Such an approach, however, is common in world politics: liberals are good, conservatives are evil; or, alternatively, conservatives are good, liberals are evil.

7. *Is the author substituting the converse for the proposition?* This is an eloquent way of saying that the author has switched the "if" and the "then" in a statement. For example, "If you use aspirin, then you will get fast headache relief" becomes "If

you get fast headache relief, then you use aspirin." A useful advertising ploy, as you can see from the example.

8. *Is the author substituting the inverse for the proposition?*
Again, this error involves an if-then statement, this time making both parts negative. The aspirin example can show the effect clearly: "If you use aspirin, then you get fast headache relief" becomes "If you don't use aspirin, then you don't get fast headache relief."

9. *Is the author drawing conclusions on the basis of similarities between things that are not very similar?* An example would be "Universal daycare, like universal happiness, is difficult to implement." Daycare is not comparable to happiness, and the difficulties of achieving the two are not necessarily comparable either.

10. *Is the author being superstitious?* In philosophical terms, superstition means concluding that, because one thing follows another, it is therefore caused by the first. An author might assert, "The general decline of the Western economy is caused by the flood of females into the work force." Although Western economies have declined since women began to be paid for their labour, there is no way of proving that this situation directly caused the decline.

11. *Is the author making* **non sequiturs?** This catch-all phrase for the most obvious errors in logical reasoning translates as "it does not follow." A statement such as "In Sweden, spanking is illegal and there is a high suicide rate; spanking must help prevent suicide" typifies the *non sequitur.*

EXERCISE THREE: CRITICAL READING
Take half an hour to read the following editorials on therapeutic cloning critically. Determine each author's approach. Can you detect intent, attitude, tone, bias, assumptions, implications? What strategies for persuasion does each writer use? Look for emotive language, down-labelling, improper use of authorities, unsupported generalizations, and so on. Are any of the errors in reasoning listed above apparent? How do the writers see the world? How have their perspectives shaped their selection of evidence? How might a third writer have presented the same facts?

Editorial #1
Ban All Forms of Cloning

The surprising news from Korea was that scientists had created a cloned human embryo, from which they were able to extract stem cells. The unsurprising news was that the destruction of said clone was approved by an ethics committee. The dirty little secret of the medical and pharmaceutical research industries is that ethical oversight provides not much ethics or oversight. The South Korean scientists gave assurances that an ethics committee had been involved. But of course. Anyone familiar with medical research knows that ethics committees are indispensable — they have the important job of wringing their hands and furrowing their brows before writing the permission slips to cross lines that heretofore were thought impermissible to cross.

Some years ago at the annual Davos international economic conference, Dr. James Watson, Nobel laureate, discoverer of DNA and head of the Human Genome Project, grew impatient with ethical questions about his genetic work, and announced that there was nothing to worry about because millions of dollars had been budgeted "to get the best ethicists money can buy." Exactly.

The ethics that the pharmaceutical industry favours is rather straightforward. Dr. Watson might be the leading zealot of the we-must-do-it-if-we-can school, but that is only because he is more frank than most of his colleagues. I remember listening to Dr. Watson at the Cambridge Union in the mid-1990s waxing eloquent about the marvels of genetic testing, suggesting that all sorts of dispositions and behaviours could be diagnosed in utero. One sensitive student spied a danger: Mightn't parents decide to abort babies "diagnosed" to be gay? Dr. Watson was nonchalant — they well might, but that's the price that has to be paid. Muffled gasps suggested that the assembly was in desperate need of the best ethicists money could buy.

Last week's cloning news illustrated how intellectually bankrupt the lucrative sub-industry of bioethics has become. Solemn assurances were given that "reproductive cloning" was a danger to be avoided, even while "therapeutic cloning" was being celebrated. The difference? The former means cloning to produce a human embryo that, if implanted into the womb, will continue to develop until birth. The latter means destroying the embryo to harvest its stem cells. To summarize the relevant ethical judgment: The embryo allowed to live should never be created; the embryo destined for destruction is ethically praiseworthy. That's the kind of tortured philosophy that requires high-priced specialists to sell.

Nevertheless, assured by the bioethics industry that all is well, the non-distinction between reproductive and therapeutic cloning has become a fashionable position. Theodore Dalrymple argued for it in these pages

72

last week, and the editors of the other national newspaper lauded therapeutic cloning while professing horror at its "scarier cousin," reproductive cloning.

A clone is a clone, yet the research industry is trying to convince the policymakers that the widespread revulsion at cloning can be overcome by the wholly artificial creation of "good cloning" and "bad cloning" categories. Governments are being urged to pass bans on reproductive cloning but to fund therapeutic cloning. The philosophical madness of such laws is obvious. "Clone-and-kill" for therapy is permitted; "clone-and-let-live" is prohibited.

The philosophical foundation for such policies runs contrary to the foundation of our human rights law. The false reproductive/therapeutic distinction has nothing to do with what a human clone is, but only what others wish to use it for. Depending on that decision, the clone becomes something that should never have been created, or something that should be quickly destroyed. This is arbitrariness of the highest order. It would fail as a valid ethical principle in any introductory course in natural ethics — leaving aside altogether what the Christian, Jewish or Islamic moral tradition might say about it.

The bioethics industry is skilled at manufacturing justifications for what the researchers want to do, always drawing the line just beyond what is possible today. Tomorrow, when the technology advances, the bioethicists return for another round of contracts and hand-wringing, before moving that line a little farther back.

Public policy ought not let those compromised hands draw the lines. At the moment, Bill C-13, the omnibus human reproduction bill, is before the Senate, having passed the House of Commons in October. The Commons debates demonstrated that there is massive support for a ban on all forms of cloning, which the bill purports to do. Now is the time for the Senate to split that part of the bill away from the more controversial sections and return it to the House. Should the government indicate openness to such a move, a comprehensive cloning ban could quickly become law.

It is now evident that the bioethics industry has become a subsidiary of the pharmaceutical companies and medical research laboratories. It is no longer credible as a guardian of the life and death matters entrusted to it. The news from Korea makes it imperative for the Canadian government to act.

- Father Raymond J. De Souza, *National Post*, 2004

Editorial #2
We Must End the Suffering

Korean scientists recently announced in *Science* that they have taken the first step toward creating genetically matched cells and tissues for transplant by growing stem cells from a cloned human blastocyst. The embryonic stem (ES) cells were created by means of somatic cell nuclear transfer (SCNT) in which the genes from donated human eggs are removed and then adult cells with all their genes are merged with the enucleated eggs.

The Korean researchers were able to coax 30 cloned embryos to develop to the blastocyst stage consisting of about 100 cells. These blastocysts are clones of the adults that donated the genetic material. They then removed the inner cell mass from 20 of the embryos and were able to establish one colony of ES cells. The cells from the inner cell mass are pluripotent, that is, they can differentiate into all the diverse types of tissues that form the human body.

Until now, no scientists have been able to grow cloned human cells to the blastocyst stage, much less create a colony of cloned ES cells. ES cells are highly desirable for transplants since they are nearly genetically identical (except for mitochondrial DNA) with the cells taken from the donor. This means that such cloned cells would be perfect transplants because they would be unlikely to be rejected by a patient's immune system. In September 2001, the U.S. National Research Council of the National Academy of Sciences' report, *Stem Cells and the Future of Regenerative Medicine*, concluded that somatic cell nuclear transfer research to create immunologically compatible stem cells like that done by the Korean researchers should be "actively pursued." That's because, as the report concluded, stem-cell-based therapies could alleviate much of the suffering of the 58 million Americans who will be struck in their lifetimes with cardiovascular diseases, the 30 million who will come down with autoimmune diseases, the 16 million who endure diabetes, the 5.5 million who will lose their minds to Alzheimer's, and on and on. Just as the medical revolution ushered in by vaccines and antibiotics vanquished many of the diseases that killed young people in the last century, stem cell therapies might conquer many of the diseases of old age in the 21st century.

Obtaining stem cells means that the blastocyst is necessarily disassembled. Pro-life opponents of cloning research claim that a human being is thus killed. If one believes that a blastocyst has all the rights of a human being on religious grounds, then there is no argument that will persuade one to permit human therapeutic research. Perhaps the best we can do in a pluralistic society is to permit those who want to take full advantage of medical advances to do so, while allowing others to refuse medical treatments that they find morally objectionable. After all, we don't force adult Christian Scientists to take medications or Muslim and Jewish people to use medical products derived from pigs.

Opponents of cloning research correctly point out that the techniques devised by the Korean researchers can be used to try to create cloned babies as well. After all, fertility doctors already implant conventionally produced blastocysts into the wombs of infertile women so that they can bear children. However, given the myriad health problems that cloned animals suffer, it would be unethical to attempt to produce a cloned human baby now.

"The goal of this research is to cure patients using their own tailor-made cells," said Daniel Perry, president of the Coalition for the Advancement of Medical Research (CAMR) in a press release. "While those opposed to medical research may argue that this work could lead us closer to human reproductive cloning, it's just not the case. There is a clear, bright line that divides reproductive cloning from somatic cell nuclear transfer and that's implantation. Without it, no new human life can be created," he added.

Opponents of human cloning research point to the numbers of human eggs that have been harvested in order to produce a few cloned cells. In this case, the Korean researchers collected 242 eggs from 16 women. They were able to culture 30 blastocysts and to obtain suitable inner cell masses from 20 of them. Only one produced a colony of self-renewing stem cells. It's clear that relying on human eggs as a way to manufacture ES cells to treat diseases will not work. Fortunately recent research on mouse embryonic stem cells indicates that embryonic stem cells can be transformed into eggs. This would mean that an endless supply of eggs would be available to jumpstart the creation of genetically matched transplants. Thus does scientific progress undercut the lurid nightmares of women being confined to human egg farms to produce eggs for tissue cloning being peddled by cloning opponents.

"While this research is preliminary, it does show what is possible and provides hope to millions suffering from life-threatening diseases and conditions," says CAMR's Perry.

Nobody said the future would be risk free, but the future also brings new opportunities to cure disease, alleviate suffering, and fend off early death. We'd be less than human not to seize those opportunities.

- Ronald Bailey, *National Post*, 2004
  (Ronald Bailey is *Reason Magazine*'s
  science correspondent)

5   Notetaking

AS YOU READ, write. A simple maxim, but one that can be profitable when applied to the task of essay research. Recording ideas and bibliographic information is, quite simply, efficient. Hours of precious day-before-due-date time can be wasted relocating that perfect quotation that captured the essence of your paper, or making one more trip to the library to obtain publication dates.

Notetaking has other advantages as well. Through writing about a text, the reader becomes more engaged than when reading passively. The act of taking notes facilitates critical reading; it demands that you understand and evaluate, continually seeking content and argument relevant to a particular focus.

Notetaking can also permit the student some distance from sources, making it a useful strategy in avoiding unintentional plagiarism. The student who takes thorough notes may not even need to consult texts during the writing of the essay, the required material having already been diligently recorded.

With all these advantages to recommend it, one would think that the craft of notetaking would be perfected early in a student's career, yet the tendency is to be sloppy at this stage of the writing process. Beginning to research by copying down bibliographic information seems tedious, and pausing to paraphrase just at the moment when meaning becomes clear is frustrating. To take notes well, therefore, requires a method so meticulous, so ritualized, that the act of jotting information down becomes second nature.

General Principles

The research process involves continual oscillation between thesis and discovery. As reading and research progress, you will revise and modify your tentative thesis. Simultaneously, however, your thesis will provide direction for your reading and notetaking. Your goal should be flexibility without chaos: do investigate new paths of information, but guard against tangents that might take you completely off course. Never work without a thesis in mind. Otherwise, texts take control of you, rather than the more desirable reverse experience.

The research process reaches forward to writing as well: the shape and size of the finished essay must be considered continually so that the specific requirements of the writing task are met. As you take notes, therefore, keep an outline in mind. The aim of notetaking is not to gather a great mass of notes, but rather to gather notes directed toward a particular end. Thinking about the various areas that must be explored to establish your argument should help you to know when you have reached the point of diminishing returns. Remember, too, that your essay has a finite length, so there is no great virtue in taking many more notes than you can hope to use. At the same time, do not skimp on space. Leave room to add comments, cross-refer to other notes, and so on.

Either index cards or ordinary paper can be used for taking notes. Many people prefer the card method, primarily because a set of note cards can be shuffled around and arranged into outline form neatly and without confusion. A second good reason for using cards is that they can be filed easily since they are all the same size and contain only one note each. Not everyone feels comfortable, however, working within the limitations of a $3'' \times 5''$ space. If you prefer the roominess of full-sized paper, use sheets of standard size so that you can keep them together.

You may choose, alternatively, to take notes electronically, using a desktop, laptop or similar device. The benefit of this method is the ability to keep your notes in one place, to store them in files with helpful names to identify themes, and to sort or search for information quickly and efficiently. But, as with all computer technology, you must remember to save often and create an electronic or hard-copy backup of your notes.

As you write or type, strive for accuracy. Your final goal is to have a set of notes that you can use with complete confidence. At the same time, bring yourself to the task of notetaking; since reading is an interaction between you and the text, you should be recording not only information and opinions, but your responses to them. Your note that Jordan's theory about continental drift seems untenable will be as useful in the writing process as the quotations and summaries you have recorded.

The notetaking method described below is based on the traditional pen-and-paper approach. You may, of course, adapt it if you take notes electronically; to that end we offer suggestions for electronic notetaking throughout the section.

Notetaking Method

1. ***Begin by writing your tentative thesis statement or description of purpose on two 3 ″ x 5 ″ cards.*** Post one of these cards on the wall above your desk for the duration of the time you spend on your essay. Keep the other one in your pocket, so that it is always available for consultation. Of course, you will probably revise your thesis as you read; continue to replace the cards to reflect the revision, and keep your spirits up by anticipating the satisfaction you will feel when you can take the thesis card down. If you use a computer for notetaking, store your thesis in a separate file on your computer. Always keep that file open, refer to it often, and revise it as necessary. This is a useful tip when you're drafting, too.

2. ***Before taking any notes on content, write the bibliographic information on its own card, one card per book, article, or other item.*** Usually for a book you will record author, title, publisher, place of publication, and date published. For an article, the name of the journal, the volume and issue numbers, the year published, and the page references will be necessary. You will, then, produce two varieties of card: one for your bibliography — sometimes called "Works Cited" or "References" — and one for the text of the essay. Note the bibliographic details exactly as they will be cited in your essay; this method will enable you to put the cards in alphabetical order and to copy from them directly to produce the bibliography or works-cited list. Include the library call number on your card in case you want to consult the book again. For a journal article, the source of reference might be useful. Also include a unique short form for the work — probably the author's last name and initials — and use that abbreviation when you take notes.

   On a computer, you will still want two files: one for the bibliographic information only and one for the notes you take on that source. The great benefit of this is that you can compile your bibliography or list of references completely as you take notes, alphabetizing it as you go. This saves a lot of time later.

3. *Write down, on separate cards, the following categories of notes.* Remember to put only one point on each card. Include the short form for the source document, and the page or line reference.

a) *Quotations.* Several restrictions apply in this category. In research papers, quotations are generally used for one of three reasons. Sometimes, the wording in a passage is so precise that it cannot be paraphrased without loss of meaning. Second, the person being quoted may be highly respected in the field and quoting him or her directly will help to bolster the case you are making. Conversely, you may wish to quote an authority in order to dispute an argument made. Finally, the stylistic qualities of the passage may demand comment. Consider the example of Churchill's World War II speech, "We shall fight on the beaches, we shall fight on the landing grounds, we shall fight in the fields and in the streets . . . ."[1] You might quote this passage, not to draw attention to its literal meaning, but to show that the manner in which Churchill expressed himself affected the public's response to what he was saying. In a literature essay, quotations are used primarily to draw attention to language, although you might also quote to show an author's point of view or philosophic leanings. A literary quotation should establish the way diction or imagery or alliteration is used by the author, not how the plot is progressing. Your own reading experience tells you that quotations must be succinct; reading nine or ten lines of quoted text is difficult and irritating. Usually, if you can't write the passage on a 3″ x 5″ card, it is too long to quote in its entirety in the essay. Always place quotation marks around direct quotations in your notes. Failing to do so may lead to unintentional plagiarism.

When you are transcribing directly, two notation conventions will be useful. The first is the square bracket: [ ]. It is used to indicate that you have added something to a quotation or changed it ever so slightly in order to make its meaning clearer. For example, if your quotation reads, "Cosmetic companies use this substance in foundation cream," you might write "this substance [whale blubber]" so that your reader will understand the reference. The second device, ellipsis dots (. . .), permits you to indicate that you have omitted a portion of a quoted passage.

---

[1]Winston Churchill, *Blood, Sweat, and Tears* (New York: G.P. Putnam's Sons, 1941) 297.

When you take notes, guard against quoting an author out of context. Introducing ellipsis dots or quoting only a sentence fragment may distort the meaning of the passage quoted. Be true to the author's intent; any other approach is dishonest.

If you are taking notes directly onto a computer, recording quotations accurately at this time will allow you simply to cut and paste them into the appropriate place in the essay later. However, don't use the relative ease of this process as an excuse to quote excessively!

b) *Facts and Figures.* Be meticulous here. Check the data you are recording carefully before you return your source to the library, so that 10,000 pounds of raw sewage doesn't miraculously become 100,000 pounds in your essay. Facts and figures, incidentally, do not need to be placed within quotation marks. The reader will understand that you have borrowed the data directly, provided that you document the source.

c) *Summaries/Paraphrases.* Probably most of your notes will be of the summary or paraphrase variety. Many novice researchers assume that if paraphrasing means putting a passage "in your own words," this can be accomplished simply by substituting synonyms for key terms. The process is actually much more complex. Proper paraphrasing depends on thorough comprehension of material, not on a thesaurus. You must read the passage you wish to paraphrase, think about it until you understand it, and then write notes as if you were explaining the idea or issue to yourself. If you have thought about the passage carefully enough, there should be no need to consult the text again while you write the summary. For example, consider the following passage:

> Studies of twins reared apart, and of foster-children whose real parents were known, have tended to confirm that environmental conditions can have a measurable effect upon the performance of children in intelligence tests. At the same time, such studies have demonstrated that the extent of any improvement which may result from a better environment is limited.[2]

---

[2]Robin E. Gregory, *A Shorter Textbook of Human Development* (London: McGraw-Hill, 1969) 57.

A proper paraphrase would approximate what follows: "Gregory's study of separated twins and foster-children establishes that a child's environment can affect intelligence, but probably only in a limited way." An improper paraphrase might read: "Studies of separated twins and of foster-children whose real parents are known have shown that environmental conditions can affect a child's I.Q. However, these studies have shown that the extent of any improvement caused by a better environment is marginal."

The first note shows the student's thought at work; the passage has been considered carefully and its principal idea deduced. The second note depends far too heavily on the original sentence structure of the passage. The same information is contained in both notes, but the latter still bears the stamp and uses the words of the original source.

As you paraphrase, strive also for accuracy. Do not confuse what you want research to show with what it does show, and do not paraphrase a point out of context. In the above passage, it would be easy to ignore the second sentence and paraphrase only the first: environment affects intelligence. Gregory, however, makes only a qualified claim. The note must reflect the author's intent.

Make sure also that you paraphrase in a manner that will permit you to attribute information properly when you write. Attribution is the proper acknowledgement of sources and actions within the main body of an essay. Your reader will want to know both where an idea or opinion came from (who wrote about it) and who the source of an action was (who did it). For example, when an essay declares that "Ontario Supreme Court Justice Jane Doe reached the decision in the 1990 court case . . . ," the reader knows the person, the person's title, and the date of the decision, and is able to assess the reliability of the decision made. If, instead, the student had written, "The decision was reached in a court case," the reader would have no way to evaluate the ruling. Likewise, in the proper paraphrase above, the reader knows that the study was completed by Robin Gregory and can evaluate the results in view of that fact. The improper paraphrase does not give the reader the same privilege. Failure to attribute is not plagiarism, but it is a serious weakness in scholarship.

d) *Comments*. As we have stressed, an essay involves interaction between you and the topic. Through reading, you will gain personal insights and will gradually develop your own opinions and perceptions. Record these insights as you read; your notes will then provide that necessary balance between yourself and the material. If you find a particular interpretation of an historical event to be the most creative and ingenious discussion you have ever read, write yourself a note explaining why. If a sociological theory helps you to understand a personal experience, write that down as well. Remember, you are reading critically, and to do that you must interact with the material.

Taking notes electronically allows you to switch easily between screens containing the following: bibliographic information, notes in the form of quotations and paraphrases, comments on sources, your thesis statement, your developing outline, and even the beginning of a draft. Try to retain control over all the files, however: it is easy to become swamped by an excess of information and end up with more work to do later. Technology should make your work easier, not complicate it further.

e) *Words that need clarification*. Make sure you understand the terms of the discussion you have entered into. If subsequent reading does not define them clearly, consult a specialized dictionary.

82

Read the following passage and consider the notes on the text which follow it. Which will be useful when the student begins to write? Which may cause problems or extra work?

> Clifford Sifton's tenure as superintendent general of Indian affairs did not occasion dramatic changes in Canadian Indian policy. He had almost no creative new ideas to offer, and most of his policy statements and administrative reforms appear to have been generated substantially within the department. It is arguable that his administrative reforms made the service more efficient, more highly centralized, and that he made a fairly steady effort to minimize the number of incompetent individuals. He left his stamp on the department in many of the leading personnel and indeed in the drastic upheaval at all levels of the staff. The changes tended to bring to power men who were if anything less sympathetic to the Indians and to place expenditure under the control of a cost-conscious bureaucracy.[3]

1. Bibliographic Card

   Hall, David J. "Clifford Sifton and Canadian Indian Administration 1896-1905."
   in *As Long as the Sun Shines and the Water Flows: A Reader in Canadian Native Studies*
   (Vancouver: UBC Press, 1983)

2. Note Card
   Hall, 137
   Hall says that Sifton had almost no new creative ideas to offer and that most of his work was generated substantially within the department.

---

[3]David J. Hall, "Clifford Sifton and Canadian Indian Administration 1896-1905," *As Long as the Sun Shines and the Water Flows: A Reader in Canadian Native Studies*, ed. Ian Getty and Antoine Lussier (Vancouver: U of British Columbia P, 1983) 136-37.

3. Note Card
   Hall, 137
   Hall is critical of Sifton, claiming that Sifton was not
   innovative in the work he did in Indian Affairs and that his
   administrative reforms brought in personnel who were probably
   not that sympathetic to natives.

4. Note Card
   Hall
   Hall writes, "Clifford Sifton's tenure . . . did not occasion
   dramatic changes in Canadian Indian policy."

5. Note Card
   Hall, 137
   During Sifton's period in office, there were few changes
   in Indian policy. Sifton was a good manager, and made staff
   changes, but the staff he recruited were bureaucrats who
   were unsympathetic to the natives.

EXERCISE TWO: PARAPHRASING
Consider the following passage:

> The expansion of Canadian aid programs beyond Asia in the late
> 1950s was undertaken to support Britain's decolonization program
> in the Caribbean and Africa. Dismantling the empire in both
> regions was a worrisome process and Britain was reluctant to
> leave its old territories undefended against possible socialist
> influences from within or without. Canada was asked to help out
> and readily agreed.[4]

Which of the following notes illustrate(s) proper paraphrasing technique?

1. Britain invited Canada to help with aid in the Caribbean and Africa,
   and Canada acted without hesitation.

2. Canada's international aid increased around the period of 1955-60
   because, although Britain wanted to pull out of Africa and the
   Caribbean, it didn't want to leave these areas entirely without support.

---

[4]Richard Swift and Robert Clarke, eds., *Ties that Bind: Canada and the Third World* (Toronto: Between the Lines P, 1982) 154.

3. Canadian aid programs were expanded after World War II.

4. Canadian aid programs were expanded to support England's decolonization program in the Caribbean and in Africa.

5. Because Britain was afraid of possible socialist influences in the Caribbean and Africa upon decolonization, it sought help from Canada in the form of increased Canadian aid to these regions.

Documentation

An academic essay, at its best, forms part of a dialogue with other scholars in a discipline: ideas are exchanged, points are disputed, facts are shared and interpreted. At the undergraduate level, the essay rarely needs to present entirely new information or ideas; rather, it brings a new mind to material already available. More concretely, no matter what your essay topic, you are not necessarily expected to uncover previously unknown information about it, but instead to contemplate knowledge already available and write about it in a manner that gives it new meaning. In Sample Essay B on development and democracy, for example, the student is not giving the instructor any fundamentally new ideas that could not be found in sources on development issues. Rather, he is using information to make a point that a reader might not be aware of: that the relationships among democracy, human rights, and development are the subject of significant debate.

Because essays do synthesize knowledge and viewpoints of others, documentation — acknowledging the source of information obtained — performs an important function in essay writing. The need to avoid plagiarism is only one of several reasons for documenting the sources of your evidence and ideas. The others are the desire to establish the reliability of the evidence you present and to provide the interested reader with the references needed to read more on the subject. Keep in mind that your essay is a dialogue between yourself and other scholars, and it should be relatively easy to determine acknowledgements.

An analogy may help you to see the correct procedure for documentation more clearly. Imagine that you play baseball, and that you are having a discussion with some of the other team members about strategies for an upcoming tournament. Everyone in the discussion will know certain facts: who plays what position, the rules of the game, the schedule of the tournament. Likewise, when you are writing an essay in a particular discipline, certain pieces of information are shared knowledge. These do not need to be documented for the same reason that you would not spend time explaining to your baseball buddies the concept of "three strikes, you're out."

However, in your baseball meeting, some facts and ideas will be known only by one person. The catcher may have developed a rationale for trying to lose the first game; if this strategy fails, you may want to remember whose idea it was. Or the pitcher may have played in the park before and remembers that hitting a home run there is next to impossible. These ideas are put forth by single voices: they are not shared knowledge and therefore need to be attributed to particular sources. Documentation in essays works in the same manner. Most geographers, for example, know that water temperature differs among the five Great Lakes, but only a few might be familiar with the causes of these differences. If such a fact were included in an essay, other geographers would want to know who determined these causes, again, to judge the reliability of the information provided and to inspect the research for themselves. Furthermore, particular sources must be given credit for concepts and opinions. The catcher's strategy was her idea: she'll be a little disgruntled if the right-fielder claims it as his brainwave after they've won the tournament.

Once you major in a subject, you will soon develop a sense of what needs to be documented and what does not. When in doubt, though, provide a reference: you will never be penalized for providing too many (although you might be advised to refine your style for future papers). Indebtedness is not in itself shameful. It is presumed that teachers and writers have something to say that will be of use to students and readers.

Our companion publication *Notes on the Preparation of Essays* describes the two main systems of documentation used in various disciplines: the traditional endnoting/footnoting method with bibliography, and the more widely used parenthetical citation with reference list. The basic difference is that, in the former, sources are listed and keyed to numbers in the body of the essay, whereas in the latter, a short form for the source is indicated in parentheses in the body of the text (where the number would be in the endnoting/footnoting system).

The parenthetical method is now accepted in most disciplines and required in many. Because the research done in different disciplines varies in objectives, the conventions of documentation vary a little as well. In the arts, scholars often recognize the beauty of the annotated footnote; the flow of the text is uninterrupted, but supplementary information is readily available to the curious reader.[5] In the sciences, where current research is constantly making earlier research results obsolete, the date of a publication figures more prominently than in the humanities, so the parenthetical

---

[5]*Thinking It Through* uses the footnoting system for precisely this reason. The footnote you are reading right now is an example of an "annotated footnote." This information would be considered tangential in the main body of the text.

method is more appropriate. The three sample essays in Appendix D illustrate various forms of the parenthetical method, but see *Notes on the Preparation of Essays* for detailed instruction on exactly how to cite what in a particular discipline.

Plagiarism

Passing off someone else's words or thoughts as your own makes you a plagiarist. This is a Greek term (*plagiarius*) meaning "someone who steals someone else's child." That the academic world should have retained a word meaning "kidnapping" to denote the offence indicates its seriousness: in the case of plagiarism the kidnapper not only steals someone else's brainchild, but also pretends to be its proud parent. (Coleridge, in one of literature's more famous disputes about who wrote what, described an essay on poetry he had planned with Wordsworth as "half a child of my own brain."[6]) The act has a further grave consequence when the work is submitted for credit: the value of the degree granted by the university is undermined every time a plagiarist graduates and goes off into the world with the school's certification of competence in a field. Therefore, plagiarism is extremely dishonourable, and can result in getting zero on a paper or in the course, or, in cases of repeated plagiarism, in debarment from the university.

At its worst, plagiarism involves presenting someone else's essay as your own, perhaps with minor modifications. It does not matter what the status of that other person is: using your roommate's essay or one you purchased from an essay-writing service or found on the Internet is as serious an offence as submitting an article by a published scholar.

Most students are not overly anxious about the intentional plagiarism described above; here, the cheating is obvious. But many are plagued by the recognition that any failure to acknowledge indebtedness for the wording used or thought expressed in an essay is plagiarism, even if the omission is unintentional and applies only to one sentence. Such anxiety is frequently compounded by the feeling that not one of the ideas in the essay is yours: all have occurred to someone else at some point.

Again, think of your essay as a dialogue among team members. The idea to lose the game is the catcher's, but the idea of agreeing with the catcher is yours. Instead of saying, "We should lose the first game," you would say, "I agree with the catcher, who says we should lose the first

[6]Samuel Taylor Coleridge, "To Robert Southey," 29 July 1802, *Collected Letters of Samuel Taylor Coleridge*, ed. Leslie Griggs, vol. 2 (Oxford: Clarendon, 1956) 830.

game (Catcher, 2004)." In an essay, you might agree with an author who believes that Trudeau made a mistake in introducing the War Measures Act; you would document the author's argument, but the fact that you were in accord would be your own idea.

Where most students err in terms of unintentional plagiarism is not in failing to acknowledge ideas, but in paraphrasing incorrectly. Stealing syntax is as significant an offence as stealing an idea because, as you know from your own writing experience, trying to phrase a point exactly is a difficult art. You can avoid this error by paraphrasing correctly as you take notes. Completely rethink a concept before you record your response to it; that way, you will be less likely to borrow word order and phraseology.

Academics are experts in reading and writing. When they suddenly encounter a plagiarized passage embedded in a student's paper, the shift in voice is as obvious to them as if they were hearing it rather than reading it. Besides, the instructors to whom students submit essays are specialists: it is their job to read specifically in the field of instruction. They often recognize plagiarized material, and are quite rightly so incensed that if they cannot identify the source of the material immediately, they will search through the literature on the subject until they do.

Now, with sophisticated search engines and plagiarism-detection tools widely available on the Internet and in software packages, the instructor's job in detecting plagiarism has become much easier.[7]

---

[7] For more information on plagiarism and on techniques for avoiding it, see Mary Ann Armstrong, *Avoiding Plagiarism*, and Tania Pattison, *Avoiding Plagiarism: A Guide for ESL Students* (Peterborough: The Academic Skills Centre at Trent University, 2002).

88

EXERCISE THREE: PLAGIARISM

The following quotations are all taken from a text entitled *Ethnicity in Canada: Theoretical Perspectives* by Alan Anderson and James Frideres (Toronto: Butterworths, 1981). Read each one and consider how it has been used in the student's paper. Which examples show plagiarism?

1. **Quotation:**

"Without realistic funding of multicultural education, as represented in second or third language instruction, ethnic-oriented histories and other textbooks, and cultural exchange programmes, it is not likely that decades of discrimination against these minorities, usually assuming the form of enforced Anglo-conformity in the schools, will be offset" (316).

Student's Paper:

Without appropriate funding of multicultural schooling, such as instruction in second or third languages, textbooks that are oriented toward ethnicity, and cultural exchanges, it is unlikely that years of discrimination, usually in the form of Anglo-conformity, will be eliminated (Anderson and Frideres, 316).

2. **Quotation:**

"Again, certain groups in Canadian society, notably the most conservative ethno-religious groups, have stressed taboos to ensure fairly rigid social control which could keep members within the fold. For example, among the Mennonite and Amish people in the Kitchener-Waterloo region in Ontario, the most conservative (Old Order) sects will not use electricity, any mechanized farm machinery, or drive cars or trucks (instead they use horses and buggies)" (45).

Student's Paper:

Anderson and Frideres note that some ethnic groups, like the Mennonites and Amish, have taboos which help to keep members within the group. They cite examples such as the refusal to use cars and electricity as instances of such social controls (45).

3. **Quotation:**
   "Canadian society, to a certain extent, exhibits some characteristics of a cultural pluralistic society. This type of system shows mutual toleration or peaceful coexistence of groups with different cultures" (297).

   Student's Paper:
   In that, for the most part, cultures within Canada are accepting of one another and abide together fairly peacefully, Canadian society can be said to be culturally pluralistic.

4. **Quotation:**
   "Because of the strong institutional completeness that existed within the Japanese community before the actions taken by the federal and provincial governments, the results of the relocation were different than for the Germans nearly thirty years previously" (270).

   Student's Paper:
   Anderson and Frideres note that "the strong institutional completeness" existing among the Canadian Japanese prior to relocation made the effects of government action different than they had been for the Germans (270).

Checklist: Notetaking

1. Record all bibliographic information before you begin to examine a source.

2. For all notes taken on a text, clearly indicate author, text, and page reference or URL.

3. Place all direct quotations inside quotation marks. If you modify a quotation, use square brackets or ellipsis dots to indicate the changes you have made.

4. As you paraphrase, ensure that you do not borrow syntax or phrasing from the original text. What you cannot put in your own words, put inside quotation marks.

5. Keep your quotations short: try not to record passages too lengthy to be used as quotations in your essay.

Following this system scrupulously will save you from both inadvertently plagiarizing and unnecessarily giving an author credit for your own ideas.

6 Prewriting

NEARLY EVERY PROFESSIONAL author describes at some point the daunting prospect of the blank page or screen. Indeed, committing the first few words to paper seems often to be the most difficult stage in the composition process, for both novice and experienced writers. The research may be complete, we may feel well prepared, but the task of writing about our subject is still onerous, since it forces us to think even more carefully and completely about the topic at hand.

Writing necessitates deep thought because it requires the student to perform a juggling act, keeping several balls in the air at once. Audience needs to be considered, as does purpose. The writer must decide what ideas to present and in what order to present them, thinking all the while about how to spell "privilege" and whether a paraphrase might be more appropriate than a quotation. Little wonder that many of us shudder at the sight of an empty page or a blank screen.

Nonetheless, the writer can learn to approach the essay so that the agony caused by penning or keying that initial word is lessened. In this chapter on prewriting, and in the two on drafting and revision that follow, we suggest strategies that should ease you into composition. Instead of beginning at word one and writing through to word two thousand, you will learn to resolve some demands before you begin to compose complete sentences, to ignore other demands until you are writing a final draft, and to use writing for discovery as well as for exposition.

Prewriting can loosely be defined as all the writing you do before attempting a formal draft of your essay. It serves several purposes. Some prewriting exercises will simply help you to understand your subject better; you will "know what you think when you see what you've said." Others will help you to realize your purpose, and the standard prewriting task — the outline — will permit you to discover the best presentation of your ideas. Overall, prewriting saves time and energy. By lessening the number of demands you must consider when writing a draft, it allows you, at that stage of the essay, to concentrate more fully on developing your thesis.

Thinking and Writing Styles

Any advice on writing must inevitably be prefaced with a qualifier: every individual thinks and writes differently. This qualification is of particular relevance in a discussion of prewriting, since not everyone needs to follow the same organizational steps to begin formal composition. The written product is, inevitably, linear; we read from the left to the right, one word after the other. Some of us think about subjects in a linear fashion, too, organizing ideas in our brain similarly to the way they are organized on paper. Such writers may see many prewriting tasks as redundant, since they can explore and arrange mentally without committing words to paper. However, others of us tend toward more holistic thinking, easily perceiving the entire argument, but not necessarily in a linear fashion. Writers at this end of the spectrum may find even a formal outline imposes too rigid a structure and will be more comfortable with mind maps and free-writing techniques. Our advice for all writers, then, is to read this chapter and experiment. Inevitably, some prewriting strategies will work well for you. Determine the extent to which you rely on linear thinking, and if prewriting strategies help you to approach that blank page with more gusto, use them every time you write.

Mind Maps

Drawing an informal and pictorial outline, sometimes known as a mind map, can be a way of freeing yourself from the constraints of sentences and paragraphs so that you can explore ideas more creatively.[1] To draw a mind map, begin by placing a tentative thesis in the centre of a blank page. Explore this thesis by drawing branches from it to represent ideas and concepts that, from your reading and research, you now associate with the thesis. As you are drawing/composing your map, create as many branches as you can, and as many twigs as possible from the branches.

---

[1]For a full discussion of mind maps, see various books by Tony Buzan, including *Use Your Head*, *Use Both Sides of Your Brain*, and *How to Mind Map*.

The mind map can be used as an exploratory method only if you push yourself to explore; restricting your thinking to the main branches will never allow you to recognize the smaller, more subtle possibilities of your topic.

A mind map for Sample Essay A in Appendix D might look something like this:

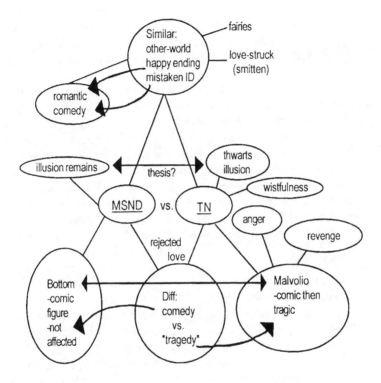

The mind map cannot show the order in which to pursue ideas, but it can suggest the direction of your thought and the connections between ideas. Once you have sketched this kind of outline, it is often possible to recognize the sequential patterns of development needed to write a coherent draft. If your mind map indicates that you have explored your subject thoroughly, it may be possible to compose your essay directly from it.

The mind map can be useful to anyone who wants to break free of the constraints of syntax, spelling, and structure. In particular, writers who cannot begin composing immediately in sentences and paragraphs, or who experience some difficulty with formulating complete thoughts when unsure of direction, will enjoy this prewriting strategy. Many software packages (some with free demonstrations available on the Internet) allow mind maps to be created (and adjusted) quickly and effortlessly; they use different shapes and colours so that you can see your ideas developing in ways that match your preferred learning style.

Free-Writing

As you know, writing is a means of thinking as well as a way of recording information. The linear structure of sentences and paragraphs forces us to explore ideas carefully, redefining, explaining, and focusing. Writing allows us to reflect on our subject, for, as Frank Smith notes, "Language permits thought to fold back on itself."[2] We write, think, and then continue to write.

Because writing provides this opportunity for reflection, it is often useful to engage in some exploratory composition before attempting a draft. Free-writing is one such exploratory route. While it permits you to think, it still provides a temporary reprieve from the anxiety of trying to obey the rules and regulations of correct writing, allowing you to juggle one or two balls instead of four or five.

Free-writing, if less disciplined, is thus more purely exploratory than writing usually is. People often find that in free-writing they can see connections that they could not make when they were trying for perfect paragraphs or sitting in silent contemplation. A session of free-writing focused on the task of jotting down the major results of a research effort can help the writer to see what thesis emerges from those results. Some writers also use it as a sort of warm-up exercise to bring what they have in mind to the surface before they begin their day's work. Even if nothing of particular interest breaks the surface, it is often reassuring for someone suffering from a temporary writer's block to know that the pen will move across the page, or the fingers across the keyboard.

Begin free-writing by giving yourself a specific time period, say ten minutes, so that you do not feel you are undertaking an ordeal, and write on the subject at hand for the whole time. It helps if you can focus on a specific aspect of your subject (not necessarily a small aspect). Write whatever comes into your mind; if "dumb, dumb, dumb, dumb, dumb" is all that occurs to you, then write that down. Do not stop to review what you have written and do not lift your pen from the paper (or your fingers from the keyboard). The idea is to keep yourself writing so that your internal editor does not have the opportunity to make you self-conscious, faint of heart, or sophisticated.

---

[2]Frank Smith, *Writing and the Writer* (New York: Holt, Rinehart and Winston, 1982) 65.

Although you may be silencing your internal editor, remember to keep a few juggling balls in the air. In particular, write honestly and thoughtfully. Merely recording information will not help you to explore. For example, if you were free-writing about your breakfast, "I ate bacon, eggs, toast, and coffee" would not show much evidence of exploration. Ask yourself why you ate what you did, and why you didn't have café au lait and a croissant. Your next line might then be, "Obviously, I prefer the American variety of cholesterol to the European." As you write, push more deeply into your topic; never use free-writing to produce only superficial information.

When you have finished, review what you have written. Sometimes you will find a good topic sentence for a paragraph that is giving you trouble. Failing that, you are still likely to find that you have managed to see your material in a different way, probably a simpler, clearer way, and your next attempt to write about it formally should be more successful. Always assume, by the way, that whatever you have free-written you must rewrite — not just fine-tune, but "rewrite" as in "rethink."

Peter Elbow has written extensively on free-writing in his books *Writing Without Teachers* and *Writing With Power*.[3] You may want to consult his texts for further free-writing strategies.

EXERCISE ONE: FREE-WRITING

Spend ten minutes free-writing with no particular focus. Simply try to find out what you have in mind at the moment.

Then spend twenty minutes free-writing with a particular focus. If you are working on an essay, one of the following might be a useful focus: the thesis, two ideas that you are having trouble connecting, or possible conclusions for your paper. If not, concentrate your attention on one of the following topics:

1. What you *don't* want to be when you graduate, and why.

2. Whom you would pick for the next Prime minister.

3. The advantages of knowing a foreign language.

4. What you do when you write an essay.

---

[3]See *Writing Without Teachers* (New York: Oxford, 1973); *Writing With Power* (New York: Oxford, 1981).

Free-Writing a Draft

Sometimes, you will find free-writing for twenty-minutes or half an hour unsatisfactory; unstructured composition for such a limited amount of time may not permit you to embrace the full scope of an essay topic. In this situation, you might want to free-write an entire draft of your paper. Provided you take the proper approach, this prewriting strategy is perfectly reasonable.

However, a few cautionary notes are required. Free-writing a rough draft can be very time-consuming; you must battle to ensure that it isn't. Set yourself a time limit. For instance, give yourself one day to write three thousand words, and stop when you have reached that goal. Remember, this is free-writing, not the composition of a first draft. You will still have to write a draft, revise it, and edit it.

Also, be sure to continue to ignore the conventions of essay writing and punctuation; concentrate on understanding your topic. There is no point in revising as you free-write, because you can't know for sure that the sentences you revise will even appear in the draft versions.

Reverse Outlines

Once you have a free draft composed, you should create an outline from it so that you can approach the first draft in an organized fashion. This is known as constructing a reverse outline. Read over what you have written; glean a thesis from it. Decide what your major points are, what your minor points are, and what will not be used in the essay at all. (The sections omitted may be fairly substantial; do not include passages simply because you have committed them to paper.) Then follow the advice given in the section below to channel your free-writing into an outline.

Outlining

Lily Briscoe, an artist in Virginia Woolf's novel *To the Lighthouse*, describes the qualities she is striving for in her painting this way:

> Beautiful and bright it should be on the surface, feathery and evanescent, one colour melting into another like the colours on a butterfly's wing; but beneath the fabric must be clamped together with bolts of iron. It was to be a thing you could ruffle with your breath; and a thing you could not dislodge with a team of horses.[4]

---

[4]Virginia Woolf, *To the Lighthouse* (Harmondsworth, England: Penguin, 1964) 194.

Like good paintings, good essays are structured so well that they appear to have no structure at all. Inspect any worthwhile essay closely, however, and you will discover, beneath the eloquent prose, the carefully wrought framework that Lily requires of her paintings. It is this framework, in fact, which makes the essay readable, for the proper arrangement of ideas and details is essential to a lucid and persuasive argument. Not all essayists work from outlines, but an essay from which an outline cannot be extracted is more likely to be baffling than brilliant. If the outline is not inherent in the essay, you may be able to fulfill your thesis, but the reader will not be able to discern it.

Many students shy away from essay outlines because they find them confusing and cumbersome, but this reluctance is often the result of a faulty approach. It is difficult — indeed, impossible — to record all the details of an argument at an early stage in the essay; you should not expect to be able to do so. Although a sketchy outline can be constructed almost as soon as a thesis is discovered, an outline expands and develops with reading and research. It is complete only at the moment before drafting begins, and may in fact be revised again if new a direction emerges during writing. Think of the outline as something you create over the course of researching and prewriting, and it will be an effective tool.

Outlines are usually understood to be a means of getting organized, and certainly spending some time outlining an essay can be practical and efficient. Ultimately, it will make the writing easier. By having the whole essay condensed on one page, you will be able to see the shape of the whole, the purpose of your paper, the relations between the main points and the supporting details, and the relative weight that should be assigned to each section. The outline therefore serves not only as a guide when you write, but also shows gaps in logic and indicates whether you need to add or omit information and ideas. In short, an outline organizes not only your writing, but also your thinking. A good outline will establish direction and topic limitation, as well as the order of paragraphs.

Methods of Organization

Eventually, you will want an outline that organizes the actual points and details you wish to include, a place to put all the research you have accumulated. However, an essay is not just a body of information; generally, it has a definite purpose that supplies shape and meaning. Before you begin putting the details of your essay into place, it is useful, therefore, to step back and consider what you are trying to create. Do you want to make a comparison? describe a process? evaluate a report? The location of details will depend on how these questions about general structure are answered. Begin your outline, then, by seeking an organizational framework — a means of considering your material that will convey its purpose clearly.

In the excellent textbook *Four Worlds of Writing*, Janice Lauer and her co-writers present four different means of organizing ideas in a paper, each suited to a different purpose.[5] We describe these methods below. Consider each method of organization carefully; one will emerge as the most appropriate for the overall arrangement of the particular concept or argument you wish to explore.

Description

Description is a much more analytical act than many textbooks suggest. When we describe, we are, quite literally, analyzing: breaking a whole into parts. For example, when we describe a person's face, we talk about colour of eyes and hair, the shape of the nose and lips, the texture of skin, and the length of eyelashes. That is, we do not talk about the whole, but about the parts that constitute the whole. We might well conclude, however, after we have described the face, that as a whole it is an attractive one.

The descriptive method of organization in an essay works much the same way. Imagine, for example, that you are writing an essay on the status of women in Canada today. Your thesis might be that the status of women in Canada today is unacceptable. To support that point, you would have to analyze the situation by describing the aspects of women's status that led you to such a conclusion. You might write

The status of women in Canada today is unacceptable.

1. It is unacceptable because pay equity hasn't been achieved.

2. It is unacceptable because women are expected to work a double day.

3. It is unacceptable because only a small proportion of women have prestigious jobs.

If your thesis seems to demand that you break an assertion into component parts in order to explain it, then the descriptive method of organization is appropriate for your paper.

---

[5]See Janice Lauer, Gene Montague, Andrea Lunsford, and Janet Emig, *Four Worlds of Writing*, 2nd ed. (New York: Harper and Row, 1991).

Narration

When you organize using the narrative method, the topic is usually being examined in terms of chronology or process. Such a method may seem very elementary, but it can allow you to understand such diverse matters as how the past informs the present, how society can be changed, how the universe unfolds. On a less grand scale, writing about the locomotion of arthropods, for example, might dictate discussing a process, so the narrative method would make sense for this paper. Similarly, writing about the Conservative Party in Canada may demand that you consider the party from its roots to its present status to establish how it has developed. Once again, the narrative method, which would permit you to consider the topic of the Conservative Party as it moves through time, would be an appropriate method of organization.

Essays on causes and effects often take a narrative form as well. In order to discuss why the Boer War occurred, or what the results of extensive use of non-biodegradables might be, it is necessary to examine the topic over time. A word of caution, however: do not confuse narrative development with producing a plot summary or a chronology. The essay must show evidence of your mind at work, selecting the most significant features of the process or discussing how one stage leads to another.

Classification

In an English essay, you might want (or be asked) to consider Stephen Leacock's *Sunshine Sketches* as a satire. The classification method of development, which usually involves putting a subject in a larger group in order to consider it more closely, would work well in this case. To classify, you need to define the larger group (What is a satire?) and then show how Leacock's text shares features with that larger group. (The book is comic; it makes fun of certain aspects of society; it invites the reader to help change those aspects.)

Comparison/contrast essays are a specialized form of classification organization. To compare any two items successfully, the items must belong to the same larger group.

When you compare, you still place the items in the context of that larger group. However, you will also proceed with an additional step. Once you have established the features both items share with the larger group, you will discuss divergent features as well. For example, were you comparing apples and oranges in terms of marketability, you might note that, although they are both readily available to the North American consumer, the orange is more appealing since its skin is easier to remove and the consumer is therefore less likely to be worried about ingesting chemicals.

Evaluation

The evaluative method of development dictates that you set a standard for your topic and measure it against that standard. Is the new housing project in your community the best solution to the problem of affordable housing? In order to evaluate, you must decide what the components of the ideal solution to affordable housing would be, and then determine whether the new housing project meets those criteria.

A final point about methods of organization: they can operate on both the macro, or global, level of essay writing and the more local level of the section or paragraph. A method of organization will provide your essay with an overall framework, but you can and should depart from it occasionally in your essay. For example, although you may be writing a classification essay about *Sunshine Sketches*, your essay could still contain a narrative passage describing the events that helped to shape the nature of Leacock's satire.

EXERCISE TWO: METHODS OF ORGANIZATION

You are asked to write an essay on the Fathers of Confederation. Invent some possible theses for this topic, and then decide the method of organization most appropriate for developing each thesis.

Repeat the exercise for the following topics:

1. The effects of purple loosestrife on wetland ecosystems.

2. The writings of Karl Marx.

3. Shakespeare's history plays.

The Formal Outline

Once you have decided on the general organizing principle your essay will follow, you can begin to think about completing a formal outline. Such a task is not always necessary. Short essays in particular often do not require an extensive outline since their brevity makes it relatively easy to see how details fit together. However, a formal outline does allow for more control in the writing of longer papers.

Any student who has done much reading about essay composition will know that there are almost as many outline schemata as there are essays. Since most of these are based on the same principle, almost any of them can be effective. An outline's usefulness depends not on keyhole or cloud shapes, or on squares and triangles, but on the effective display of a paper's priorities.

Whatever sort of outline is used, it must establish relations between main points and subordinate points, between subordinate points and details, and between all points and the thesis. Above all, the outline must provide a sketch of the development of the thesis, not just a list of headings. It is vastly more useful to the writer if the line of thinking that the essay follows is displayed than if only the ground to be covered is detailed. To be succinct: the outline should reflect the thesis, not just the topic.

Essay outlines can take a variety of forms, and if you decide to write an outline you should adopt one that fits most appropriately with your preferred learning style. What we discuss below is the linear essay outline; however, the model is adaptable, and the same principles apply to a less linear outline that relies on graphics or highly visual mind-mapping techniques.

The formal essay outline is hierarchical and linear. It depicts the main stages in the development of the essay in their relation to each other and in the order in which they will occur in the essay itself. Its linearity — first this, then this, then this — makes it easy to write from because it matches the linearity of the essay form. The skeleton of a formal outline should look something like this:

Thesis Statement:

    I.
        A.
            1.
            2.
    II.
        A.
            1.
            2.
        B.
            1.
                a.
                    i.
                    ii.
            2.

This outline establishes relations among the ideas in two ways: through a numbering scheme, and through the way in which points are displayed on the page. Related ideas are grouped together under main categories (I and II in the diagram), and within each of these categories, general (A and B) and specific (1 and 2) ideas are recorded. These divisions can be further broken down (a and b; i and ii), although caution should be exercised at this point — too much specificity often only delays the writing of a paper; you also need a certain amount of flexibility so that the outline develops and changes as you write.

The most expedient way of constructing an outline is to decide first what the main divisions of your essay are, then the secondary categories, and then, in turn, the further subdivisions. Your thesis may suggest the main divisions to you; thinking about methods of organization will also help. With practice, you will discover that most essays under 5,000 words fall naturally into two to four main divisions. An outline that proposes seventeen main divisions signifies that you have not yet found the connections between your ideas and are veering away from analysis toward the listy, catalogue-style approach.

However rigidly disciplined the outline might seem in format, developing it should be a flexible process. Think of it as the preliminary sketch that a painter makes before committing oils to canvas: use the outline to try to visualize the essay you have in mind but have not yet thought your way through. Try to imagine its basic shape, the order of sections, the organizational method. As you proceed through your research, keep improving on your outline. You can go through six or eight versions of an outline in very little time, chopping here, adding there, rearranging the whole order until you have the best structure possible. You can plan a nicely balanced paper by using the left margin for estimating the space requirements of the various sections of the essay: five hundred words for this major division, two hundred for that minor one, and so on. Indeed, a good deal of planning can be accomplished with a formal outline, but don't allow a plan of action to prevent you from exploring new ideas. Remember that the outline is more useful if you sketch it in pencil than if you carve it in stone. Changing or at least monitoring your outline as you go enables you to be more aware of the essay-writing process and maintain control over it as you write.

Creating the Formal Outline

As we have said, an effective outline must display the essay's thesis. To show how the thesis is established through outlining, let's consider the example of Sample Essay A. The thesis of the paper is not expressed in one sentence; instead, the entire introduction develops the thesis, which can be paraphrased as something like this: Although *Twelfth Night* and *A Midsummer Night's Dream* are alike in many ways, they differ primarily because of two characters — Malvolio and Bottom — whose differences make *Twelfth Night* less a purely comic play than *A Midsummer Night's Dream*.

On a broad, rather general level, the main headings of an outline for this paper would look like this:

I. Similarities in theme: the two plays
II. Similarities in character: Malvolio and Bottom
III. Differences in character: Malvolio and Bottom
IV. Differences in theme: the two plays in general

Such a list of headings is of little use. Although it does show the order in which the main points will be put forward, it does not establish the development of the thesis; the student has not declared specifically what each section will do to contribute to supporting the overall thesis. A slightly more developed outline would be more helpful:

I. There are three important themes shared by the two plays: other-world settings, happy romantic endings, and mistaken identities.
II. The two characters also have much in common: they are both, unlike other characters in the plays, unlucky in love.
III. The significant difference between the two plays lies in the two characters' different attitudes toward their romantic situation: Bottom is unaffected, while Malvolio becomes a tragic figure.
IV. The difference between the characters is the crucial factor in distinguishing the plays from each other: *MSND* remains entirely comic, while *TN* takes on a more serious tone.

The statements made for each section of the paper in this outline provide the student not only with direction, but also with perspective. The outline actually depicts the development of the thesis. The writer employs the tried-and-tested comparison-contrast method of classification, which enables her to maintain tight control over both the general (i.e., on the level of the plays themselves) and the specific (i.e., on the level of the two characters under discussion) aspects of the thesis.

This type of outline can also help you to direct your research, should you need to conduct any. The main headings above would be formulated at an early stage in the writing process — after some careful readings of the plays but before any detailed analysis. Once aware of the argument to be made about the points above, the writer could direct attention to a very close comparison of the chosen themes and characters. This creates the narrow focus that is required in any paper and helps the writer avoid vagueness or sweeping generalizations.

From the broad outline above comes, for many writers, a narrower, more detailed outline of the particular points that constitute the thesis. Often the detailed outline will include a paragraph-by-paragraph sketch of the logical development of the argument; sometimes it is less detailed, depending on the proposed length of the paper. Other writers will simply take the broad outline as a springboard into their first draft, perhaps fine-tuning or elaborating upon their outline between successive drafts. This interplay of outlining, drafting, and revising can also identify possible dead ends or tangents in the essay's logic. If a particular point is going nowhere, or going in the wrong direction, or cannot be supported, this problem will often be exposed by the outline. Such points should either be reformulated or eliminated completely. (Of course, having a large number of these points would suggest a complete reworking of the essay's thesis and direction.)

Here is a more fully developed outline of Sample Essay A in Appendix D. The numbers in square brackets refer to the paragraphs in which this information is presented in the essay.

Thesis: Although *Twelfth Night* and *A Midsummer Night's Dream* are alike in many ways, they differ primarily because of two characters — Malvolio and Bottom — whose differences make *Twelfth Night* less a purely comic play than *A Midsummer Night's Dream*; *Twelfth Night* thwarts illusion, and acquires wistfulness, whereas *A Midsummer Night's Dream* does not.

I. There are three important themes shared by the two plays *A Midsummer Night's Dream* and *Twelfth Night*:
1. other-world settings — both plays are set in illusion:
   a. *MSND* has fairies and make-believe;
   b. *TN* shows a reversal of the natural order, e.g., Olivia, Viola *[2]*
2. happy romantic endings — both plays are typical of romantic comedy, love = star-struck illusion:
   a. in *MSND*, the potion from the flower;
   b. in *TN*, characters are instantly smitten *[3]*
3. mistaken identities or situations — again typical of romantic comedy:
   a. in *MSND*, shown through the Demetrius-Helena-Hermia and Lysander-Helena-Hermia triangles;
   b. in *TN*, Viola-Sebastian, Olivia confusing Cesario and Sebastian, Malvolio mistaking Olivia's love for him *[4]*

II. The two characters also have much in common: they are both, unlike other characters in the plays, unlucky in love:

    1.   Malvolio's love for Olivia in *MSND*;

    2.   Bottom's love for Titania in *TN [6]*

III. The significant difference between the two plays lies in the two characters' different attitudes toward their romantic situation:

    1.   Bottom is unaffected by his rejection:

         a.   he considers it a dream;

         b.   he participates in the mechanicals' performance *[7]*

    2.   Malvolio is deeply affected and becomes a tragic figure:

         a.   he is put in prison and is appalled at this treatment;

         b.   the play turns from comedy to tragedy; Malvolio promises revenge; reality replaces illusion *[8]*

IV. The difference between the characters is the crucial factor in distinguishing the plays from each other:

    1.   *MSND* remains entirely comic:

         a.   feelings are superficial;

         b.   no strong emotional reactions in evidence;

         c.   the world of illusion remains intact *[9]*

    2.   *TN* takes on a more serious tone:

         a.   perspective changes as play progresses;

         b.   difference between comedy and tragedy (General Introduction);

         c.   theme of two faces: Cesario, Malvolio *[10]*

EXERCISE THREE: CREATING THE OUTLINE

The preceding outline, like most plans that writers work from, is useful but not perfect as a sketch of the development of the thesis. Ask yourself how it might be polished by considering the following questions: Is it apparent from this outline how the thesis will be demonstrated? Do all points and subpoints support and develop the essay's central idea? Is the organizational method apparent and appropriate? In what areas might the essay be expanded? Could any section be combined, shortened, or eliminated? You will want to compare the outline with the essay itself.

EXERCISE FOUR: CONSTRUCTING THE REVERSE OUTLINE

1. Do a reverse outline of one of your own essays in linear form. First, look for the thesis statement, then the main divisions of the paper. Include the mini-theses for each main section, and work toward three levels of subdivision (I.A.1). You should end up with a sketch of the argument of the paper. Alternatively, use another student's essay or a published essay for this exercise.

2. Construct a reverse outline of Sample Essay C in Appendix D. Critically examine the outline you have created and suggest ways in which the development of the argument in the essay could be modified.

Checking the Formal Outline

Get into the habit of looking for three main qualities in the outline as you refine it: stride, analysis, and substance. These qualities can be verified by a simple visual check — the look of the outline — and they are more easily seen in a formal outline than in a mind map.

First, stride. Do the main divisions of your thesis move somewhere? You should be taking mental steps from section to section, not inching your way along.

Second, analysis. Say your thesis has three main sections. Ask yourself, "If I show my reader that the mini-thesis for section one is supported, and for section two, and for three, will my reader see that my main thesis is supported?" Then check within each section in the same sort of way. By this means, you are checking the basic analytical integrity of your thesis. You are seeing, in other words, whether the pieces into which you have broken your main thesis are the ones needed to reconstruct the whole. If not, either some of the pieces belong to another essay, or your thesis still needs refining. The outline and the thesis must fit together perfectly.

Third, substance. Are your assertions backed up by evidence? Look at the level of your outline that deals with detail. Do you find sufficient reference to your material to back up the assertions you are making about it? You can write a witty, insightful, even elegant essay, but if you do not show your reader how your insights illuminate the material itself, you will not be rewarded for your efforts. You will, in fact, seem more interested in your own cleverness than in the topic you are exploring.

Checklist: Outlines

1. Have you placed your thesis at the top of your outline? Does every main division and subdivision advance your thesis?

2. Does your outline emphasize important ideas and details by giving them adequate space? Check for gaps and bulges; as a general rule, look for evidence of biting off more than you can chew (too little support, reader getting suspicious), and worse yet, chewing more than you've bitten off (too much support, reader getting sleepy).

3. Are your details, examples, and more specific statements subordinated to the general statements in the outline?

4. Are ideas of the same level of generality ranked equally in your outline?

5. Is there a good mix of main headings and subordinate points? If you find that you are listing a large number of points as main headings, you may not be generalizing enough.

6. Do your main divisions suggest the direction of your thesis?

7. Are the ideas arranged in the most effective order?

8. Is your outline concise? It is important that the outline contain enough detail to enable you to move easily to the first draft; but it must also be brief enough to give you a picture of the whole. If you find that your outline has grown to three pages, write another one-page outline to be sure that you are clear about the main lines of your essay.

EXERCISE FIVE: CHECKING THE OUTLINE
Assess one of the outlines that you created in Exercise Four, above, or one that you have produced for another essay of your own. Does it have the qualities of stride, analysis, and substance? Are there gaps or bulges? What changes would you make to the outline if you were to rewrite this paper?

Not employing an outline makes your essay a high-risk endeavour in one of two ways. Some students go the "work to the deadline" route: they use drafts as outlines and therefore have a tendency to produce an eccentric and misshapen third draft that becomes the final draft because the essay is overdue. Others, slightly less diligent, produce awkwardly structured first drafts that become final versions because they cannot bear to scrap the result of so much work. You may be one of the lucky few who are quite capable of producing an organized paper without benefit of an outline, but if the words "poorly organized" appear anywhere in your instructor's comments, take heed of the suggestions in this section.

Once you have achieved an outline that seems strong and genuinely useful, the process of writing the essay can begin. Try not to write mechanically from the outline; doing so will give your essay a stilted tone and cramp your thinking. If, in the course of writing, a brilliant idea occurs to you that you had not anticipated at the outline stage, cheerfully change your plans. Only be sure to revise the outline, and check that your altered course still gets you where you want to go.

7 Drafting

ANN BERTHOFF HAS described the composition process as an act of "making meaning," a turn of phrase that indicates precisely writing's duality of purpose.[1] On the one hand, words are the symbols through which we externalize and shape the process of thought. We think through writing, "making meaning" for ourselves — making sense of our subject, discovering its significance to us. But while writing permits us to explore, it also allows us to communicate — to "make meaning" for a reader. We write to discover what we think, but we also write to tell others what we are thinking.

These dual (and sometimes duelling) purposes figure prominently in the composition of a first draft. At this point, the writer is still in search of meaning. Although one necessarily begins a draft with at least a premise (or hypothesis) and probably a formal outline, in the process of writing one must be allowed the freedom to test and examine and expand, to pursue a natural course of exploration and investigation. The essayist, like the scientific experimenter, must observe the effects of the method employed, both anticipated and unforeseen. Conclusions must arise from the process of wriggling free from the restraints of preconception and prescription even if (and especially if) those conclusions undermine or redirect the tentative thesis or purpose.

---

[1]See Ann Berthoff, *The Making of Meaning: Metaphors, Models and Maxims for Writing Teachers* (Upper Montclair, NH: Boynton/Cook, 1981).

At the draft stage, however, the writer will also begin the task of conveying ideas to an audience and will move away from a personal and private record of exploration toward a form of writing that "makes meaning" for an unseen reader. Written language, shaped as it is into phrases, sentences, paragraphs, and essays, conveys meaning through its organization. The conventions of the introduction and the paragraph, or the rules of punctuation and syntax, serve like the movements of dance to choreograph the motion of the mind: they draw patterns of meaning out of our initial, insinuating gestures toward thought by arranging and directing, ordering and scripting chaos. The conventions of written language help thought to emerge from language, just as the choreographer coaxes the dance from the dancer.

The most practical way to view a draft, then, is as an *essai*, an attempt at both thinking and writing about your topic. You will want, in thinking, to get your ideas on paper so that they can be examined, reconsidered, revised. You must therefore write quickly, recording ideas as they occur to you, exploring and refining thought. However, in terms of the finished product, you also want a draft you can work with, a draft that has some meaning: it may have a few tangents, but it should not be entirely tangential; it may depart from your outline, but it needs some semblance of organization.

As far as the thinking is concerned, you are on your own. No guide to essay writing can help you invent your ideas, other than by encouraging you to use writing as an opportunity for exploration. But in this chapter we can help you with the second objective. We will show you how to put together a first version of your essay that will be of use to you when you commence the hard task of revising and truly making meaning for your reader.

Composing The Draft

Before you can grasp the components of a first draft, you must understand how the finished essay works to make meaning for the reader. The key word here is *unity*. To persuade a reader that you understand a topic, you must produce a unified essay, just as a choreographer would labour to ensure that, despite the twenty people moving in different directions on the stage, the audience still perceives the elemental whole of the dance.

Another analogy may help you to see how important unity is. Imagine, for a moment, that you want to establish your understanding of the mechanism of a clock or watch. You begin by disassembling the watch into its component parts. When the watch is in fifty separate pieces on your desk, *you* can see how it operates. But to convince anyone else that you understand the mechanism, you must put the pieces back together, refashioning it into a unified, ticking whole. Likewise with an essay.

Although "analyze" means to "break into parts," breaking into parts is never enough. You must synthesize as well by reuniting the disparate elements. In this creation of a whole, your understanding of the subject is established.

Creating unity involves not only combining parts to form a whole, but also showing clearly and distinctly the relation between parts. We have all had the experience of watching a music video in which incongruous elements are juxtaposed; we wonder, "Just what was the connection between the attractive woman and the aquarium?" As artists, many video producers deliberately try to evoke the elusive quality of dreams, where the connection between ideas can be guessed at but not stated with certainty. The intent is often to subvert the world of cohesion and order.

Essays are not music videos; when written to form, they are card-carrying members of the world of cohesion and order. Helping your reader to understand how you got from one point to another and why you are writing about what you are writing about is crucial to making meaning. Furthermore, your route of exploration must be one that can be followed easily and that makes logical sense. An undergraduate essay is usually not the place for experiments in narrative technique: stream-of-consciousness writing and flashbacks are taboo.

By the final draft, then, the relation of the components of the essay to each other and to the paper as a whole should be self-evident and unambiguous: unity should be achieved. However, the student who attempts to produce a unified, cohesive essay in a single attempt often falls victim to that dreaded disease of composition: writer's block. The reason for this lies in the fact that creating unity is not an isolated task, but an ongoing part of the writing process. As we revise and edit our drafts, we work again to establish the relation between parts and whole. Moreover, unity must be achieved on several planes: at the global level of sections and paragraphs, but also at the more local level of sentences and punctuation. To retain your ability to explore while still creating a piece of work that will be useful to you, contemplate unity as you draft, but only at the level of the sections and paragraphs of the essay. Considerations are broader here, but they are also less numerous, so the flow of your writing (and the activity in your mind) will be less inhibited than if you worried about word choice, punctuation, and tone. Because one begins writing with words and sentences, thinking about them too much during drafting can keep a writer stuck forever on the first paragraph. Better to give some thought to sections: that way, you can hold the essay in your mind and you have an approach that propels you forward, rather than leaving you beached on page one.

A final gentle reminder before you begin: relax. Give some thought to what follows, but do not aim now for a completely unified product.

Remember, as well, that although "making meaning" for a reader is important, you should also be discovering meaning for yourself at this point. Don't concentrate on unity so rigidly that you forget to think deeply about your subject.

Drafting the Sections

Very few essays, no matter what their thesis, cannot be subdivided into major sections. As we consider a topic, we almost automatically break it into pieces of accessible size. For instance, a student writing on the vegetation in a particular area would certainly devise some categories in which to place ideas — trees, flowers, fruits, and vegetables, perhaps, or spring, summer, and fall vegetation. The reader, likewise, prefers demarcated sections; information is more easily retained when perused in manageable chunks. Since sections serve both the writer and the reader, you should think while you draft about what they are and how they relate to each other. In terms of the content in your paper, you will find that the way you arrange ideas into sections can help your reader understand your material better. In addition, you will discover that certain sections of the essay — the introduction, conclusion, and transitional sections — have as their primary function the task of helping the reader achieve the unity of a paper.

Methods of Organization

If you have produced a formal outline for your essay, you will already have contemplated unity at the section level: the methods of organization discussed in the chapter on prewriting — description, narration, classification, and evaluation — are means of showing how sections of a paper are related to one another. Using a particular method to establish the connections between the sections of your essay will make it easier for both you and your reader to predict what comes next and to fit the sections together.

Most theses can be developed according to any one of the four organizational methods: your choice should be based on which fits your thesis best. For example, if your topic were the dangers of nuclear energy, each of the methods would be a possibility. Were you trying to argue that nuclear energy stations should be abolished, you might use the descriptive method, articulating the reasons why these stations are dangerous. If your intent is to show how the dangers of these stations have increased since World War II, a narrative method would be appropriate. You might, on the other hand, be arguing that nuclear stations aren't nearly as dangerous as coal mines, and the classification method would work well then. Finally, if you were trying to establish the strengths and weaknesses of nuclear energy, you might use the evaluative method, envisioning what the ideal energy supply would be and judging nuclear energy against that standard.

No matter what method of organization you select, remember that it need establish only the logical connections among the sections of your paper; it is not necessary to maintain the same organizational approach within a section.

Rhetorical Strategies

Once you have decided on an organizational method, you will have sections, but you may need to make a further decision about the effective arrangement of those sections. This decision is a rhetorical one in that you choose the most persuasive ordering of your ideas. Rhetorical strategies provide unity by giving the writer another means of establishing how ideas fit together; used effectively, they can allow you to demonstrate your sense of what the reader should see as primary, secondary, or tangential.

Rhetorical and organizational strategies work together to make meaning. One need not override the other. For instance, let's return to the descriptive organization of the dangers of nuclear power. You know you will talk about three dangers, but which one should come first? The answer lies in a consideration of rhetorical arrangement. The following examples of common rhetorical methods illustrate different possibilities for the effective arrangement of sections.

General to specific

The topic is approached on a general level first, and more specific details follow. Were your topic the dangers of nuclear energy, you could begin by discussing the problems caused by radiation in general, and then discuss the particular dangers present within a nuclear power station. Using this arrangement can help you to maintain your focus throughout.

Specific to general

Here, the details appear before the more general comments. You would begin by discussing specific health hazards faced by power-station workers, and finish by considering the broader environmental implications of nuclear energy. The rhetorical advantage is that the generalizations seem inevitable by the time you make them; the disadvantage is that it is more difficult to maintain and control your focus if you arrange your ideas in this way. You must be sure that the specifics have an intrinsic interest, that you do not confuse and consequently irritate your reader, and that the conclusion gains from being held in suspense.

Climax

The points appear in order of least to most important to the argument. For instance, if you consider the day-to-day hazards in a nuclear plant more dangerous to workers than the very unlikely possibility of a nuclear explosion, you might choose to deal with explosions first. Your intent must be clear to the reader from the outset when a climactic arrangement is used; otherwise, the ideas presented will only confuse. The rhetorical advantage of a climactic arrangement becomes even clearer when you consider that you would never use an "anti-climactic" approach, i.e., beginning with the real dangers of nuclear power and ending (with a thud) with the improbable nuclear explosion.

Increasing complexity

A variation on the climactic model, this pattern arranges points from the simplest to the most complex. Since you begin by establishing the points that are easiest to prove, this arrangement allows you to advance your argument relatively quickly and thereby establish a strong momentum early in the essay. In an essay on nuclear plants, your simplest point would probably be the consequences of a nuclear explosion, since they are obvious and drastic. You could begin there and work through to more intricate, and probable, pernicious problems.

Many well-organized essays are written without a deliberate application of these methods of organizing material; indeed, debating about which one to choose can lead to even greater frustration and, again, writer's block. However, it is useful to be familiar with them. Consider the variety of methods of organization and rhetorical arrangements possible when you are wondering where to start and which section to write next, and include arrangement of ideas among the qualities you check for when you are revising the first draft.

Introductions, Transitional Paragraphs, and Conclusions

Another objective in drafting is to consolidate ideas, and particular sections of the essay focus almost entirely on this goal. Introductions can begin to achieve unity by preparing the reader for the sections that follow. Well-written transitional paragraphs, which announce and explain a shift in thought process, will provide unity within the body of the paper. Conclusions, if they refresh the reader's mind about purpose and implications, can augment unity where it counts most: at the end of the paper, when the reader is also drawing conclusions about the effectiveness of the essay.

Introductions

Probably more text gets deleted and paper gets thrown in the recycling bin when writers are attempting introductions than at any other time. Getting those first few paragraphs down can take Herculean effort; we hesitate because we are daunted by the magnitude and difficulty of the task before us, and we fear that unless we find exactly the right way to begin, we will botch the job entirely. Fear and loathing and basic laziness aside, we are usually not very good when we begin a new piece, often because we are unsure where we are going. Eventually, your introduction will become the key to your essay: by reading it, the reader will be thoroughly prepared for the maze of intellectual and creative thought about to be experienced. But when you haven't gone on the journey yet, it is fairly difficult to map where you have been. If you are unable to produce a creative introduction the first time around, use your initial effort to help maintain unity through the draft. You know your major sections: outline what they are and how you intend to consider them.

Then, move on to the body of the essay. There is little point trying to achieve a creative introduction in the first draft if one doesn't occur to you easily; through the writing process, you may move away from your initial intent and have to revise all those clever turns of phrase anyway. What you want at this stage is a working introduction, one that will keep your draft intact but that does not drain all your creative energy in its production. Once the body of your essay exists — in draft or final form — you are in a better position to write the definitive introduction to it. Knowing where you will end up can help you map the route you'll take to get there.

Transitional Paragraphs

Once you begin drafting the body of your paper, you have started an exploratory journey that can lead you into all sorts of quagmires, animal traps, and enchanted forests. Some of these will prove to be worthwhile and valuable digressions, but you must keep your initial task in mind: get that dragon slain. Otherwise, overall unity will disintegrate.

One sound way of maintaining this unity is through the use of transitional paragraphs. When you have finished a section of your paper, pause in the production of content and use a paragraph to regroup your thoughts. Discuss what you have written and what you are going to write; decide on the connection between the two. Because such paragraphs force you to consider more carefully the direction you are taking, they are useful in, perhaps even essential to, the composing process. Also, if they are strategically placed between each of the major sections of your paper, they keep your reader aware of your thesis and its development.

Begin each transitional paragraph by summing up the section you have just written, elaborating on its significance to your paper. Then, explain to

116

your reader and yourself how it connects to what will follow. Is the next section more important? Less important? Does it develop an idea further? Conclude the transitional paragraph by introducing the next section of your paper; name what is to follow.

Conclusions

By the time you are concluding your first draft, you probably will have begun to realize the route of exploration your paper has taken. This route may be the one you foresaw in your outline, or it may diverge slightly from it. In the process of writing, for example, you might discover that two ideas you thought unrelated have strong parallels. If these parallels are worth investigating, do not eliminate them simply because they do not match a preconceived thesis. Rather, make a note to revise your thesis in order to include the new points.

Eventually, your conclusion will serve to unify the entire paper, pulling together the ideas contained and pointing out their implications. In a first draft, try to get at the bare bones of that unity. Think seriously about what you have written thus far, about the substance of each section, and summarize what it all means. Don't worry too much about grand rhetorical flourishes; if those are necessary, there will be plenty of opportunity to invent them at the revision stage. What you want now is a sturdy conclusion that permits you to understand what you have written, one that can act as a guide at the level of global revision.

A Note on the Use of "You" and "I"

The three essay sections described above — introductions, transitional paragraphs, and conclusions — are the areas of an essay most suited to establishing your own authorship. So feel free to use "I" to identify yourself as the driving force behind the logical organization and progression of the paper. Phrases modelled on "Now that I have illustrated/discussed . . . , I will turn to . . ." can be useful in reminding the reader that a human being is behind the words on the page. They also help to convince the reader that you believe strongly, not only in your thesis, but also in the way you have chosen to present it. There are other times, however, when it is natural and sensible to use the first person: to make a transition from reporting someone else's thought to asserting your own, or to modulate the force of a piece of writing, whether to tone it down or to make it more assertive: "Although Hobson's analysis is intelligent, I would maintain that his premise is wrong." First-person statements should always be used in moderation, of course, and never gratuitously; they are always preferable, however, in modern writing to stodgy, almost archaic third-person formulations such as "the author of the present paper" and "this writer." At the same time, the whole essay is yours, which means that whenever you say "I feel," your readers might wonder whether you have more or less confidence in this statement than in any other in the essay.

It is risky to address the reader directly. Readers accustomed to a more formal relationship with their writers find "you" overly familiar. The practice is especially objectionable when the writer is presuming the nature of the reader's response: "When you read Lady Macbeth's lines in the sleep-walking scene, you want to cry your heart out." Such presumption is to be avoided no matter what the conventions of your discipline regarding "you" and "I." In this book, for example, we have opted for the familiar "you," but have tried to avoid the presumptuous one.

If you are in doubt about when (or if) to use the pronouns "I" or "you," check with your instructor. Look in recently published journals of your discipline to check on whether and how the first and second person are used. New disciplines have challenged many of the traditional academic conventions, and it may be perfectly legitimate to write certain kinds of essays using "you" and "I." When in doubt, however, avoid both.

Drafting Paragraphs

Thinking about sections provides a bird's-eye view of the essay, but when we are actually writing, it is often hard to see the whole enchanted forest: the trees of content keep getting in the way. As you produce a first draft, then, you need to think not only about the essay as a broad whole — about the larger sections — but also about how meaning is made from the bottom up, about how the smaller parts fit together to produce the essay.

If the sections of an essay provide meaning by dividing the thesis into easily understood components, then the paragraph can be seen as developing bits of ideas into units large enough to make meaning clear. The paragraph is the basic unit of essay composition; it is like a little essay in itself. Taken together, all of the paragraphs in the essay are a visual representation of the thinking process by which the writer demonstrates his or her thesis.

As with sections, therefore, the principles of unity emerge as crucial. Each paragraph must be a unified entity; that is, it must be about only one main idea. Furthermore, the main idea must be developed through details, examples, and explanations so that the reader can see how the sentences within the paragraph form that entity. Finally, there must be connections made both within and between paragraphs so that the reader can move easily through one paragraph and on to the next. Do not expect your paragraphs to meet all of these criteria in a first draft. In the revision process, you will have plenty of opportunity to tighten cohesion and to make a paragraph more unified. For the time being, just consider the following general information about paragraphs and try to apply it. Do not, however, focus on paragraphs to the extent that you curtail the free flow of your thought.

The Controlling Idea

The paragraph develops one small idea just as the essay develops one large idea, and each new paragraph signals a shift in focus, whether in time or place, in approach, in subject, or in idea. Thus, a paragraph break does more than give the reader a little rest; it allows both reader and writer to see the structure of the essay.

What a paragraph needs, therefore, is a controlling idea — a principle or concept that dictates the content of the passage. Quite simply, you should be able to sum up in one sentence what a paragraph is about. The summation need not actually be a part of the paragraph (we refer to it as a topic sentence when it is), but all sentences in the paragraph should have a direct connection to it. For example, the controlling idea of this paragraph is the definition of a controlling idea. Often it is better — less contrived — for the controlling idea of a paragraph to become évident from the logical development of the sentences it contains rather than for it to be stated directly and unnaturally in the first sentence.

Developing the Controlling Idea

A controlling idea will help you achieve a unified paragraph, but developing that idea is also important. A controlling idea on its own does not constitute a paragraph; it needs to be fleshed out with relevant details, examples, implications, and qualifications. If paragraphs were not developed in this way, writers would run through their general ideas like soothsayers in such a hurry to proclaim their wisdom that they have no time to be interesting, clear, or persuasive.

A paragraph in an academic essay, therefore, is rarely only one or two sentences (although such short passages may be used occasionally to summarize, emphasize, or provide a transition from one main idea to the next). About one hundred to two hundred words is a more appropriate length.[2] Some paragraphs will be longer than others, some shorter. Don't fret about length as you draft, but check the size of your paragraphs when you revise.

---

[2] You will notice that many of the paragraphs in this text are very short. We consciously chose small controlling ideas so that our readers would not have to work too hard to understand each point. The controlling idea of an essay paragraph, however, can be much larger than those in the paragraphs of *Thinking It Through*.

Making Connections Clear

Since each new paragraph signals a change in focus, each is a potential source for lack of cohesion in the essay. Strive as you write to make clear how each paragraph connects to its predecessor. If you fail to do this, you cannot expect the reader to make these connections: you may find, when your essay is returned, that you have been misinterpreted.

Internally, paragraphs must also move smoothly from one idea to the next; the reader should be able to see how each sentence relates to the controlling idea and to the other sentences around it. In other words, the paragraph must advance the main idea without losing the reader; it must have internal cohesion.

Another aspect of connecting ideas within paragraphs is connecting your own prose to the prose you quote: incorporating quotations. Many students display anti-social mannerisms in their style of quotation. Instead of deftly integrating a pointed phrase into their own prose, or offsetting a longer passage to focus on it in comments that precede and follow, they stick a colon at the end of a sentence, slap the quotation down and say no more about it, as though the very act of including the quotation speaks for itself.

The whole point of quotation is not to stack up evidence, courtroom style, but to establish for your reader that, in writing your paper, you are engaging in a scholarly debate. Your intent is not to quote authorities but to show the reader that you have listened to them and that you feel that they often have worthwhile things to say. It is your voice the reader should hear, but within your paper that voice should be speaking to the other voices, the other authorities on the topic.

To achieve this dialogue, you must incorporate quotations into your own prose. Introduce the quotation by letting the reader know your opinion of it: do you agree? disagree? feel the author is only partially correct? feel that this example of poetic diction is exemplary? After the quotation has been recorded, comment further by telling the reader what was significant in the passage quoted. Draw attention to the particular phrase or idea you wish the reader to see in the passage. The aim, once again, is internal unity: ensure that your quotation works with the rest of the paragraph to create a unified whole. Don't quote too frequently, and don't always quote at length. Choosing just the right amount to quote directly can help you make your point more effectively. See Chapter Five for ways to do this at the notetaking stage.

✣   ✣   ✣   ✣

You may realize by now that this chapter on writing differs from the others in *Thinking It Through* in that it contains no checklists or exercises. These omissions are deliberate. As we wrote in the introduction to this chapter, a first draft is an attempt at an essay, not something that can be considered complete, or something that can be made perfect with practice. Inevitably, the draft will fall short in some ways: the organization is weak, or the transitional paragraphs are missing, or the paper has a thesis in the body other than the one stated in the introduction. These imperfections should not concern you during drafting. You can save extensive deliberations for revision: at this stage simply roll up your sleeves, flex those fingers, and write. Exercises and checklists for the topics covered in this chapter — particularly sections of the essay and incorporating quotations — can be found in Chapter Eight.

8   Revising and Proofreading

THE ULTIMATE AIM in essay writing is to produce prose in which meaning is clear, both to the writer and to the reader. However, it is often impossible for writers to know exactly what they mean until they see what they have written, and this is why revision is such an important aspect of the writing process. Imagine an argument in which you were not allowed to retract or recast a thought, or a first draft that was not full of scratched-out words and inserted phrases. Difficult, isn't it? Because creative people constantly evaluate and reconstruct their ideas and their expression of ideas, writing inevitably incorporates revision.

Sometimes, it is best to separate these two acts artificially, to put off the assessment and reworking of writing until after a first draft is complete. If you continually rethink every thought before recording it, or if you struggle to achieve clear and graceful language in a first draft, you run the risk of writing very little. So write the first draft quickly if you can, leaving yourself time to revise carefully after putting it aside for a day or two. With the passage of time, it will be much easier to see your writing as another reader would see it. Also, with the benefit of the distance that a few days can provide, you will be more likely to see what you actually wrote instead of what you meant to write.

Above all, remember that you should not feel that you are a failure if you need to rework your first draft. The best writers revise their work constantly, although students often find this difficult to believe. To most of us, good writing seems to have sprung from the writer's mind fully formed; it appears too natural, too obvious and graceful to have been achieved through the process of revision. However, seemingly effortless prose, like seemingly effortless dance, is rarely just that; the easier the performance appears, the harder the performer has worked. Revision is the way a writer works at his or her writing.

When discouraged about your own "natural" ability as a writer, remember that many great writers could more accurately be called great revisers. George Orwell's brother-in-law, with a disrespect common among relatives and close friends, attributed Orwell's success as a writer to hard work, not to talent. As he said, "You can't put in all that amount of work and not get somewhere."[1]

Actually, the act of revising should make you feel powerful and in control of your writing. While your first draft was an attempt to make meaning that was guided only by your outline or by your creative vision, your revised essay is built on your own writing; each revision of this writing should bring you closer to your intentions. While convinced of this fact, a student might still be confused about how to begin revising an essay. To revise a paper means "to look again" at the essay you have made, not just to tinker with what you now have in print. The ability that computers give you to revise, proofread, and correct without having to handwrite an entirely new draft at each stage is obviously an advantage to you, but it also makes it easier for you to tinker rather than to address global, structural concerns. Not only do people who compose using computers (nearly everybody these days) plan less than people who handwrite their texts, but computers also encourage excessive attention to low-level concerns. Because computers make it easy to fiddle with the sentences and paragraphs of essays, and since a computer's screen shows only a small portion of a complete essay at one time, students often neglect the most significant improvements they can make to their papers. They spend their time endlessly tidying up sections of their work without discovering how these sections might be rearranged and more closely connected to make up a whole.

When you revise you are looking for discrepancies, discrepancies between what you intended to write and what you actually wrote, between what your audience expects and what you actually deliver. Therefore, the first task of the revision process is to print a hard copy of your essay draft; reading the hard copy through is better than looking at the partial view of your essay on your computer screen while you compose. Examine the whole of your essay before its parts. Revising at the global level first will

---

[1] Audrey Coppard and Bernard Crick, *Orwell Remembered* (London: British Broadcasting Corporation, 1984) 129.

prevent you from merely changing particularly glaring errors and help you to truly "re-see" your work.

Next, you should scrutinize the sections of your essay: the paragraphs, the introduction and conclusion. Computers make reordering paragraphs easy to do, but before you cut and paste, you must read your first draft carefully with this question in mind: do these sections work together to create a coherent and cohesive unity? If your sections are not working or flowing together, ask yourself what you must do to achieve these qualities when you rearrange the essay on your computer. What emerges should not be choppy; the natural flow of the argument must be maintained. What you must do, therefore, is not simply put your ideas in the best possible order, but also work at reconstructing the logical connections between these ideas and at making these connections apparent to your reader. It may be necessary to add a transitional sentence to some paragraphs; you may want to change the transitional words you have used to ones more appropriate to your new pattern of development. Finally, print a second revised hard copy and read this over twice: first, to double-check for overall structure, unity, and coherence, and, second, to revise the sentences of your paper so that their structure, diction, and grammar adequately communicate your ideas.

Revising the Whole

As with drafting, revision begins by considering the global level of your essay: its topic, thesis, and organization; the voice you have used to present your ideas.

Revising for Topic, Thesis, and Organization

First read the draft in its entirety on a hard copy, pretending that you had no hand in its production. Determine what the topic of the essay is, and see if this topic has been focused on quickly enough. Decide what the main point or thesis of the essay is. It is not sufficient simply to restate your original intentions regarding topic and thesis at this point, since you may have diverged from them. You must try to see and judge your essay as a stranger would. This objective view can be achieved in several ways, all of which require that you ask yourself what the essay really amounts to. Producing a reverse outline could help you see the essay's structure and thesis clearly. You might imagine you are describing the essay to a friend. You could try to think of a situation, event, or thing that exemplifies the central concern of the paper and then test your expression of topic and thesis against this example. Writing a paragraph of three sentences beginning "What this essay is really trying to get across" might also prove useful. It is important that you give yourself some distance (a few days, ideally) between finishing writing and beginning to revise.

Once you have decided what your first draft is actually about, what its main thrust is and what it veers toward, you have to decide if its direction is appropriate. First of all, are you satisfied with the essay's topic and emphasis? Second, does its focus adequately meet the expectations of your instructor or of your writing assignment? Finally, examine the essay's main point and ask yourself what the significance of that point is. Does the whole essay leave you asking "So what?" If so, the essay's topic or thesis needs revision. Even if your essay does answer this question implicitly, ensure that, at some point, it answers it explicitly.

After assessing the significance and appropriateness of the essay's topic and thesis, look to see that these components are clearly expressed and developed. Inexperienced writers seem to digress because they fail to show how the details they recount relate to their papers' major concerns. Make sure that everything in your essay is connected to your topic and advances your thesis. Also, guard against wandering away from your topic and providing your reader with irrelevant information. While you should present all relevant facts and theories adequately and fairly, all that you present must be related to your essay's particular focus. Every general statement you make, including your thesis statement, should be both supported by evidence and connected with the essay as a whole.

If the first stage of revising at the global level involves looking at an essay's topic and thesis, the second stage should include a detailed evaluation of the paper's organization. Now is the time to recall what the chapters on prewriting and drafting taught you about methods of organization and rhetorical strategies. You should examine your essay to see if its underlying outline is suitable and apparent. Check your reverse outline against your original outline, if you produced one, and against your draft to see what omissions or additions you made. Describe the organization of your first draft and ask yourself if a different organization might suit your purpose better. Finally, be sure that your use of transitions and key terms reveals your essay's pattern of development.

Revising for Voice

Every writer strives to find a recognizable and representative voice, a unique style and tone that adequately reflect self. Struggling to achieve this worthy ambition may take a lifetime, but even a novice writer can revise his or her voice so that it is consistent and conforms to the expectations of the academy.

To determine whether you have written your first draft using a consistent voice, read the whole essay aloud (or ask a friend to read it to you). Do you sound like a cheerleader in one section, a skeptic in another, and a fence sitter in the next? Does your prose vacillate between familiarity and remoteness, casualness and formality, or between nonchalant humour at one point and sedate serious-mindedness at another? Obviously, these possible inconsistencies in voice have been exaggerated, but most writers, especially when they are working on an unfamiliar writing task, find it difficult to achieve a regular, harmonious style and tone.

Revising with an eye to the suitability of voice dictates making judgments about audience and purpose. If your purpose is to write an expository essay describing a particular event, circumstance, or process, you would probably lean toward an accurate, unambiguous style and a formal tone. It is hard to imagine a playful, personal voice in an essay on the formation of coral reefs, although such a voice might be entirely appropriate for a paper on the role of the cartoon hero in Canadian cultural mythology. A writer whose main purpose is to persuade might also attempt a closer relationship with the reader by using a more familiar tone. In all cases, the decision to use a less formal voice should be made after considering whether the intended audience would be open to such informality.

Decisions about what readers might consider appropriate are often difficult for students to make. Generally, assume that you are writing for an informed scholarly audience composed of your classmates and your instructor. You must awaken this audience's intellectual curiosity, and you must, at least, make an attempt to meet the conventions of scholarly discourse. What are these conventions? Well, they are constantly changing — which makes them hard to define. But they all can be listed as choices that essay writers must make at the global level of revision: whether to use the first and second person ("you" and "I"), gender-neutral language, the active or the passive voice, the "historical present."

You and I
See pages 116-17 in Chapter Seven for a discussion of this topic.

Gender-Neutral Language
Writing practices regarding the use of male terms as generics reflective of both men and women have been challenged and changed. The argument that "he" is generic, not male, that "he" means "he or she" already, is no longer acceptable to many academics. These scholars argue that the word "man" does not mean both man and woman, that "policeman" does not mean policewoman too, and that the body of paperboy does not contain the rib that is a papergirl. They feel that "he" does not imply "she too, of course": the image that comes quite sensibly to their minds is incorrigibly, persistently male. In fact, studies indicate that "the pronoun *he* and the noun *man* and its compounds occur much more frequently as sex-specific

or ambiguous expressions than as true generics."[2] These studies suggest that the tradition of using male words as generics is inaccurate and in need of reform.

Some professors and writers, however, argue against the use of cumbersome gender-neutral language. They believe that regardless of how well intentioned linguistic devices that include women might be, some are unnatural, unlovely, and an assault on the elegance of the English language. Especially offensive to their ears and eyes are alternative forms requiring slashes or parentheses like s/he, (s)he, he(she), and him/her. These forms do look and sound awkward because they have no clear counterpart in spoken language. However, is it not better to be ungraceful than unjust?

Can the real concerns of both groups be reconciled? Yes, prose can be revised to demonstrate gender accurately, inoffensively, and elegantly. First of all, however, avoid the generic use of "he" and "man" where such a use is unjust, incongruous, ambiguous, or unacceptable to your audience. The social sciences and the sciences have generally adopted the female-inclusive forms of pronouns to enhance the accuracy with which research in these fields can be communicated. If a physical anthropologist is writing about a paleolithic female skeleton, for example, precision would dictate the use of the feminine singular personal pronoun. Also, it would be ridiculous to refer to such a skeleton as an excellent specimen of Neanderthal man. In other disciplines, the practice of including women is preferred by some scholars, acceptable to most, and reviled by a few. Check the journals.

There are many strategies that include women in the English language without offending the grace or elegance of prose. When writing about a person who may be a woman or a man, you could simply use "he or she" or "she or he." Try not to repeat these combinations too frequently, however, as a page littered with such phrases is often difficult to read and too general in tone. The use of double pronouns should also be avoided when revising a sentence liberally peppered with singular pronouns. The following sentence would be an ungainly thing indeed if revised in this way: "He must admit his thievery and show himself reformed before we trust him again with earwigs that are not his." In such cases, rewrite the sentence to cut down on the incidence of pronouns: "The thief will neither regain our trust nor touch our earwigs except by admitting guilt and proving reform."

---

[2]Francine Wattman Frank and Paula A. Treichler, *Language, Gender, and Professional Writing: Theoretical Approaches and Guidelines for Nonsexist Usage* (New York: Modern Language Association of America, 1989) 146.

Another option is to alternate masculine and feminine pronouns, using "she" occasionally and "he" at other times. You must take care that this strategy does not confuse your reader and that your alternating use of "he" and "she" does not accidentally display sexual stereotypes. It would be embarrassing indeed if you used this option in an attempt to be evenhanded and discovered that you had referred to nurses, teachers, and librarians as females and to doctors, professors, and entrepreneurs as males. As a matter of interest, the handbook that many of our parents reared us by, *Dr. Spock's Baby and Child Care*, was revised using this strategy to avoid sexist language.

Sometimes it is possible to revise sentences that use the generic "he" by recasting them into the plural. Since "they," "them," "their," and "themselves" are not sex-specific, this type of revision allows for gender-neutral language. The sentence "A writer must examine his heart to determine if his prose is honest" would become "Writers must examine their hearts to determine if their prose is honest." It can be dangerous to revise in this way if your sentence contains more than one plural noun. Ambiguity of pronoun reference could result. In the following sentence, "they" could refer either to "people" or to "doctors and nurses." "People schooled in the ways of doctors and nurses know that they can cope in a hospital setting." Also, make sure that you do not violate current grammatical logic by referring to singular nouns using plural pronouns. And remember, too, that there is no such word as "themself." Another alternative is to revise your sentences so that you use the impersonal pronoun "one," the first-person pronouns "I" and "we," or the second-person pronoun "you." Considerations of your purpose and of the formality of your writing task should determine which pronoun is most appropriate. You have already been warned of the dangers of using "you" and "I" in academic prose. The only reason not to overuse "one" is that it might make your writing seem overly formal and stuffy. Any of these pronouns, however, allows you to avoid using the generic "he."

Regardless of the objections of some to the use of gender-neutral language, you probably should revise your writing with an eye to eliminating sexist nouns and pronouns. Barring a return to the days when universities were for men only, we can assume that most scholars will eventually accept "her" on the page beside "him"; after all, they got used to seeing her in the classroom beside him.

EXERCISE ONE: GENDER-NEUTRAL LANGUAGE

Revise the following two passages so that women are included in the language used.

1. Narcissism represents the psychological dimension of this dependence. Notwithstanding his occasional illusions of omnipotence, the narcissist depends on others to validate his self-esteem. He cannot live without an admiring audience. His apparent freedom from family ties and institutional constraints does not free him to stand alone or to glory in his individuality. On the contrary, it contributes to his insecurity, which he can overcome only by seeing his "grandiose self" reflected in the attentions of others, or by attaching himself to those who radiate celebrity, power, and charisma. For the narcissist, the world is a mirror, whereas the rugged individualist saw it as an empty wilderness to be shaped to his own design.[3]

2. Being read fairy tales by a parent is one of the most enriching experiences in childhood. First, the mere presence of a parent is important. Reading is one of many ways in which special moments can be shared with the very young child. More important than the physical presence of the parent is his role as mediator between the child and the fairy story. A mother or father makes a child feel safe in the presence of giants, hungry wolves, and wicked stepsisters. Yet there is an even more subtle kind of reassurance given to the child by the reading parent. Psychologists tell us that the basis of most fears in early childhood is the child's emerging independence from, and subsequent guilt about, his parents. By being present as the child imaginatively kills off wicked stepmothers and replaces them with Prince Charmings, a parent can indicate to a child that he may freely indulge in his fantasies of independence. The child can be assured that his mother or father will survive his aggressive fantasies, and respond to his simultaneous need to be dependent.

---

[3]Christopher Lasch, *The Culture of Narcissism: American Life in An Age of Diminishing Expectations* (New York: W.W. Norton, 1979) 10.

Active/Passive Voice[4]

The matter of using active or passive verbs occasions less contention among instructors. Most agree that students should maintain the active voice in their essays except in circumstances where the passive is more effective. Such a consensus has probably been reached because there is agreement that, when the focus requires, the subject of a sentence should present the person or thing most directly responsible for the action or state denoted by the verb. So, if your focus is on who won World War II, then "The Allies won World War II," not "World War II was won," which is uninformative, nor "World War II was won by the Allies," which is awkward.

Use the passive voice when your focus is on the person or thing affected by or receiving the action denoted by the verb. So, if your focus is on the war rather than on who fought it, then "World War II was fought in Europe, Africa, Asia, the Atlantic, the Pacific, and the Mediterranean," not "The antagonists fought World War II in Europe, Africa, Asia, the Atlantic, the Pacific, and the Mediterranean."

When your focus requires the passive voice and also makes mentioning the person or thing responsible for the action unnecessary, use the short passive, as in the sentence just recommended (the short passive does not indicate by whom the action is performed). On the other hand, when your focus requires the passive voice and makes the person or thing responsible for the action relevant, use the long passive: "Germany was weakened by constant guerrilla attacks." The emphasis here is on Germany as the entity affected by the action, but the performer of this action is relevant.

As you can imagine, then, context and the meaning you intend play a large role in your decision concerning your focus, and therefore in your choice between the active and passive voices. To guide your judgment further, examine the following excerpt from the writing of a major literary scholar, the late Northrop Frye:

> Those who are concerned with the arts <u>are often asked</u> questions, not always sympathetic ones, about the use or value of what they are doing. It is probably impossible to answer such questions directly, or at any rate to answer the people who ask them. Most of the answers, such as Newman's "liberal knowledge is its own end," merely appeal to the experience of those who have had the

---

[4]Verbs that express action originating with a "doer" and affecting someone or something else are called transitive. These transitive verbs have two voices: the active and the passive. In the active voice, the "doer" is the subject of the sentence: "The cow jumped over the moon." In the passive voice, the subject of the sentence is the person or thing affected by the action expressed by the verb, not the "doer" of this action: "The moon was jumped over by the cow."

right experience. Similarly, most "defenses of poetry" are intelligible only to those well within the defenses. The basis of critical apologetics, therefore, has to be the actual experience of art, and for those concerned with literature, the first question to answer is not "What use is the study of literature?" but, "What follows from the fact that it is possible?"[5]

In this paragraph, all the sentences after the first are in the active voice because the focus requires this voice. But why does Professor Frye begin the paragraph with a sentence in the passive voice (the underlined)? The answer is that in the first sentence his focus is on those affected by the action. And he uses the short passive because the identity of those who ask the questions is general and therefore unnecessary to mention.

Exercise your judgment according to the guidelines we have offered. Our advice is that you not think of the choice between active and passive as an independent, technical matter. Doing so is likely to misguide you or to stall your writing. While writing, follow your sense of context and your intended meaning; then refine your judgments when you revise. Try to use the active voice whenever your focus requires because in this case it will give your sentences efficiency and drive. But neither voice has a monopoly on directness.

The Historical Present

Instructors also generally agree that students should use the "historical present" when describing events in a work of literature or when discussing the intent and impact of authors or scholars, even when the work of literature is from the distant past or the authors and scholars are dead. It is more accurate to use the present tense in these circumstances because the arguments put forward by scholars, and the characters presented and the scenes depicted by novelists, poets, and dramatists continue to live in the present. An added benefit is that the use of the present tense makes for immediate and lively writing.

Consider how awkward Sample Essay A would sound if its author did not use the historical present frequently in references made to Shakespeare's plays. If the essay had been written using the past tense, this excerpt would read as follows:

---

[5]Northrop Frye, *Anatomy of Criticism: Four Essays.* 1st paperback ed. (Princeton, NJ: Princeton UP) 10.

Both plays were set in illusion. *A Midsummer Night's Dream* included fairies in its cast and the title suggested a dream-like world of make-believe. In *Twelfth Night*, Shakespeare again used the title to indicate that Viola's world was different from the every-day world. Twelfth Night was a time when the natural order was reversed, and revelry or the "Lord of Misrule" became sovereign. Olivia fell in love with a boy so young his voice was yet to change (1.4.32-3), and Viola and her brother met and did not recognize each other until they compared notes about moles on their father's face (5.1.242-3). Both plays existed in very similar imaginary worlds.

Compare the passage above to the original version (the second paragraph in Sample Essay A). Do you notice how direct and clear the original is? In the rewritten version, the past tense renders the analysis remote and ineffective. Check your draft to see that you have employed the historical present whenever its use brings strength and immediacy to your voice.

EXERCISE TWO: THE HISTORICAL PRESENT
Examine the three sample essays and pinpoint examples of the use of the historical present. Recast some of these passages into the past tense. Compare these revised passages to the originals, and contrast the effectiveness of each. While you are working, check the sample essays for instances where the historical present might have been used but was not.

Checklist: Revising the Whole

Topic and Thesis

1. What is the essay about? What is its topic and its central concern or thesis?

2. How significant is the essay? Have you demonstrated this significance?

3. Do the essay's topic and focus fulfill the expectations of the audience?

4. What promises does the essay make to its readers? Are these promises kept?

5. Is the purpose or the thesis of your essay stated clearly and developed sufficiently?

6. Does everything in your essay relate to your topic and thesis, and have you demonstrated these relations?

7. Have you provided sufficient and accurate facts, references, quotations, examples, and illustrations to support your thesis and all other general statements?

8. Have you commented on how the evidence you provide is significant to the development of your essay?

Organization

1. How is your essay organized?

2. Will the pattern by which your essay develops be clear to a reader? Can you underline specific words and passages in your paper that help a reader see this pattern?

3. Would a different rhetorical or organizational strategy suit your purpose better?

4. Do you indicate which ideas are of major importance and give these ideas proper emphasis?

5. Are there gaps in the logical development of your essay that need to be filled? Are there intrusions that sidetrack the main thrust of your paper that should be removed or rearranged?

6. Have you used transitions to show the relations between the points you make?

Voice
1. Have you maintained the same voice throughout the essay? Try to personify this voice. Does it suggest that of a particular type of person? Who?

2. Are you the person you want to be in this essay? Do you sound authentic? Would a different voice suit your purpose or your audience better?

3. Is your writing overly formal or informal? Do you use "I," "we," and "one" appropriately?

4. Will the way you have referred to gender please or offend your audience? Did you follow the conventions of your discipline when deciding how to use gender-neutral language?

5. Have you used the active voice as much as is suitable? Are your verbs expressive and strong?

6. Have you used the historical present when discussing scholarly works and when describing the events recounted in literature? Is your voice immediate and direct?

Revising the Sections

By now, you should have a good grasp of your essay's overall purpose, structure, and voice. With the most global revisions complete, you can begin shaping the sections of your paper — the paragraphs and the introduction and conclusion — to reflect your carefully considered goals.

Paragraphs

When you wrote a first draft, you probably considered the general principles of paragraphing, using each paragraph to develop what you thought to be one idea. It is difficult, however, to produce perfect paragraphs at the draft stage, especially if you are trying to write quickly. All too often, stray sentences will enter into your prose — and stay there — unless you revise carefully once you have finished drafting. What you want, ultimately, is a series of paragraphs, all of which develop one particular idea clearly. Your first step in revision at this level involves what is called glossing, determining the single idea being developed in each paragraph. To do this, read each paragraph. Try to sum up, in a sentence or less, what the central idea of the paragraph is. Then, read the paragraph over again. Are there any sentences that do not relate to this main point? Quite often, there will be. These should be eliminated, either by deleting them, placing them in another paragraph where they do fit, or reworking them so that their relevance to the controlling idea is made clearer. You may discover that your paragraph has two controlling ideas; in that case, produce two separate paragraphs, each with a controlling idea.

Once you have identified the main idea of each paragraph, you must ensure that you have developed it properly. Controlling ideas, like thesis statements, are assertions. As such they are not self-evident and need support. For this reason, as we have said before, a paragraph is rarely less than one hundred words. If your paragraphs are too short, ask yourself if you have developed the idea adequately. Perhaps you are presenting isolated points as paragraphs. If your paragraphs are too long (more than a page), you may be generalizing too much, or simply stringing ideas together. Look for ways of separating ideas or of breaking the main idea of long paragraphs into several component parts that could be developed in smaller paragraphs. Another possibility is that you might have been overzealous in your provision of evidence. Enough is enough.

Each paragraph must also read as a unified whole, advancing the main idea without losing the reader. There should be no difficulty in understanding how one sentence relates to another. Here are some tips on how to achieve paragraph unity and coherence:

1. *Pronouns*

   You can use pronouns to maintain coherence while avoiding repetition. When you use a pronoun, make sure that it is obvious which noun it represents. A pronoun stands *pro* — "on behalf of" — a particular noun, not a group of words or a whole sentence. Avoid using "it" or "this" to refer to a sentence or idea. Vague pronoun reference is one of the principal sources of confusion in student essays.[6]

2. *Repetition*

   It is not wrong to repeat a word several times in the same paragraph. In fact, repeating key words can tie sentences together clearly. However, if you suspect that hearing the word "liberalism" again would bore the reader, you can use a synonym or summary word to avoid repetition and still sustain coherence by preceding it with a demonstrative adjective: hence "this political philosophy" or "that movement emphasizing liberty." If you use synonyms, be sure that they are exact, not just any thesaurus-style alternatives. Do not substitute "power" for "authority" or "rights" for "privileges" merely to break the monotony. Note that this paragraph contains the words "repeat," "repeating," and "repetition": retaining the root word but modifying its grammatical form is another way of avoiding monotony without losing clarity.

3. *Transitional Words and Phrases*

   These words and phrases can join ideas together in a sentence, sentences together in a paragraph, and paragraphs together in an essay. They are words such as "equally," "subsequently," and "conversely," or phrases such as "as a result," "for example," and "in conclusion." Even this incidental list shows how useful transitions are in unifying paragraphs. By linking ideas and, more important, by signalling the logical relation between the ideas they link, transitions indicate the main point of a paragraph and reveal how subordinate points relate to it. See Appendix B for a list of transitions grouped according to the logical relation they signify and their function.

---

[6]See Pages 159-60 for a further discussion of pronoun reference.

136

Read the paragraphs below. Find the controlling idea of each paragraph, name the methods of organization used in each, and show how each is given coherence.

1. There were three groups which caused the weakening of the Shah's position. First there were the mullahs, religious leaders who lost not only land but also spiritual and secular influence during the Shah's reign. Second there were the Western-educated businessmen, professionals, and intellectuals, who were outraged by the Shah's denial of civil and political liberties and disappointed in his economic programs. Then there were the students, whose concerns were diverse. Some sided with the mullahs. Others sided with the middle class in their dissatisfaction over economic progress. Still others were dedicated to establishing the outlawed Marxist Party.

2. In Placentia Bay, Newfoundland, fish have been found floating on the surface of the sea, red with the phosphorus lost from a chemical plant. In Lac Dufault, Quebec, researchers have found high levels of copper, lead, zinc, cadmium, arsenic, and mercury from mining operations. In Pinchi Lake, British Columbia, there are no fish at all as a result of mercury pollution. Industrial wastes are upsetting nature's balance in every region of this country.

3. Beneath the epidermis lies a much thicker portion of the skin — the dermis. This consists basically of connective tissue, a type of material that is found throughout the body, filling in the interstices between the other structures. Here it is essentially a tough, felt-like material made up largely of a multitude of interlacing fibres. This tissue constitutes the greater amount of the thickness of the skin; prepared animal hide, such as the leather of our shoes, is entirely connective tissue.

4. During the five years following the passage of the Potlatch Law in 1884, no arrests were made. Then in August 1889, a man was arrested and convicted of holding a potlatch. Three weeks later, however, the case was appealed and the prisoner discharged. In making his judgment, the Supreme Court Justice who heard the appeal questioned whether the law could be enforced at all because it did not adequately define "potlatch." The problem which he raised was only one of the problems which made the Potlatch Law difficult to enforce until it was omitted from the legislation in 1951.

137

EXERCISE FOUR: PARAGRAPH STRUCTURE AND TRANSITIONS WITHIN PARAGRAPHS

Combine the following sentences into a paragraph. Make any necessary changes, such as inserting transitional words, to make the arrangement smooth. Note how the impact of the paragraph changes as the arrangement improves, even though the ideas and evidence are the same:

Differences derive from differences in character, and they are the reason *Twelfth Night* thwarts illusion, and acquires wistfulness, whereas *A Midsummer Night's Dream* does not.

They differ in their portrayal of illusion, and they show different relationships of character to it and to its effects.

There are many similarities between Shakespeare's comedies *A Midsummer Night's Dream* and *Twelfth Night*.

Both involve other-world settings, happy romantic endings, and mistaken identities.

Shakespeare's comparative treatment of the two characters Malvolio and Bottom is a significant locus of these contrasts between the two plays.

In *A Midsummer Night's Dream*, Bottom is a uniformly comedic figure. In *Twelfth Night*, on the other hand, Malvolio is both a comic and a tragic figure.

EXERCISE FIVE: PARAGRAPH STRUCTURE AND TRANSITIONS WITHIN PARAGRAPHS

Examine paragraphs one, two, and three in Sample Essay B. How could the transitions and links between ideas in those paragraphs be improved?

Incorporating Quotations in Paragraphs

As you know, if quotations are to be effective in your writing, they must be carefully worked into your own sentences and paragraphs. Sometimes at the draft stage it is difficult to think quickly about how a quotation might be positioned within your own prose. Since the tendency when we draft a paper is simply to plop quotations down where they seem useful, revising to ensure that quotations are introduced, commented on, and related to the controlling ideas of the paragraphs in which we have placed them is usually necessary. Also, the grace and argument of a sentence or a paragraph containing quotations should not be interrupted.

The note below is a direct quotation from Annette Tromly's *The Cover of the Mask: The Autobiographers in Charlotte Brontë's Fiction*. It would be presented in the form of a set-off quotation: indented on the left side, with no quotation marks. Following this presentation are several examples illustrating how part of this passage may be incorporated into a writer's own sentences.

> Jane's most important relationship exists in that strange imaginative mid-region half-way between illusion and reality. The genesis of the relationship goes as far back as Gateshead. Enclosed in the Red Room, Jane is torn by opposition and dominated by her literary imagination.[7]

1. Tromly argues that "Jane's most important relationship exists in that strange imaginative mid-region half-way between illusion and reality."

2. According to Tromly, "Jane's most important relationship exists in that strange imaginative mid-region half-way between illusion and reality."

3. "Jane's most important relationship" occurs, in Tromly's view, "half-way between illusion and reality."

These examples simply report Tromly's ideas, but they do so smoothly, and without abandoning the reader. The next two make a direct comment on the material quoted:

4. Tromly is wrong when she argues that "Jane's most important relationship exists in that strange imaginative mid-region half-way between illusion and reality."

5. Tromly argues convincingly that Jane Eyre's attachment to Rochester "exists in that strange imaginative mid-region half-way between illusion and reality."

The last example places Tromly's ideas in context by referring to other researchers' treatment of the same topic:

---

[7]Annette Tromly, *The Cover of the Mask: The Autobiographers in Charlotte Brontë's Fiction*, English Literary Studies 26 (Victoria: U of Victoria P) 53.

6. All Brontë scholars agree with Tromly on one point: "Jane's most important relationship exists in that strange imaginative mid-region half-way between illusion and reality."

There are many ways to introduce quotations. When you see that you have repeated "X writes" for the umpteenth time, consider an alternative from the following list:

> according to
> in the opinion of
> as X adds, admits, affirms, argues,
>   believes, confirms, declares,
>   insists, mentions, proposes, reports,
>   reveals, states, suggests, thinks,
>   verifies

EXERCISE SIX: INCORPORATING QUOTATIONS IN PARAGRAPHS
Examine how quotations are used in the following paragraphs taken from student essays. Do these quotations enhance a reader's understanding of each paragraph's controlling idea? Are all quotations introduced and commented on sufficiently? Decide which examples use quotations most effectively and gracefully, and which do not. Defend your decisions.

1. As in the past, Wilkes did not hesitate to capitalize on the popular support he had. But his motives remained consistently selfish, as his own words attest:

    > I owe money in France, am an outlaw in England,
    > hated by the King, the Parliament, and the bench of
    > bishops . . . . I must raise a dust or starve in a gaol . . . .[13]

    Implicit in these words is an outright admission that if there had not been a danger of ending up in prison, Wilkes would not have put himself in front of the cause of liberty.

2. Not surprisingly, the wide number of bases on which a nation can be founded often leads to a variety of conceptions of the nation in any specific case. Africa serves as an excellent illustration of this. Minogue refers to pan-Africanism as "an imprecise aspiration based on geography and colour." On the other hand, the nation of Nigeria found itself confronted with the Biafran separatist movement.

140

3. Overwhelmed by the apparent change in Hamlet after he has assumed his "antic disposition," Ophelia cries:

> O! what a noble mind is here o'erthrown:
> The courtier's, soldier's, scholar's, eye, tongue, sword;
> (3.1.158-59)

It is clear that Goethe missed the total Hamlet and by this failure his understanding of the play was substantially limited. He saw only the gentleman and scholar of which Ophelia speaks but disregarded the equally significant "soldier" whose "sword" completed the line.

4. If these were the only references to war in the play then we might have a difficult time defending Hamlet as a man of strength. But he himself makes several allusions to battle strategy and fencing, an indication of his familiarity in such matters:

> For 'tis the sport to have the enginer
> Hoist with his own petar: an't it shall go hard
> But I will delve one yard below their mines,
> And blow them at the moon . . . . (3.4.206-09)

In direct reference to the ensuing conflict between himself and Claudius, Hamlet remarks on "the pass and fell incensed points / Of mighty opposites" (5.2.61-62).

Transitions between Paragraphs

While it is important to revise the structure and contents of paragraphs so that they exhibit unity, it is equally important at the revision stage to make sure that each paragraph connects to the one preceding it and to the overall thesis of the paper. Writers can make use of the following transitional strategies to ensure that connections are clear for the reader.

1. Connect the preceding paragraph with the new one by reminding the reader of your thesis as you begin the paragraph.

Example: Clearly, then, our obstetrical procedures have not kept pace with our knowledge of infant psychology. Especially serious has been the early separation of the new-born from its mother.

2. Use a key word from the preceding paragraph.

Example: Our increased attention to psychological tendencies such as bonding [discussed in previous paragraph] should lead to new hospital procedures.

3. Use a transitional word or phrase. (See the previous explanation and the list of transitions in Appendix B.)

4. Begin the paragraph with a sentence that glances backward to the last paragraph and forward to the new one.

Example: If the last decade has witnessed many changes in theory [subject of preceding paragraph], practice has not kept pace.

EXERCISE SEVEN: TRANSITIONS BETWEEN PARAGRAPHS
Examine the essay on democracy and development (Sample Essay B). How could you make use of the techniques described above to improve the links between paragraphs?

Introductions

There are other, special kinds of sections that demand attention at the revision stage. One such section is the group of paragraphs that constitute your essay's introduction. This section will almost invariably need to be revised, since it is likely that, when you first drafted it, you really didn't know what you were introducing. Also, be assured that most of us lack confidence when we begin to write. The experience of fumbling and straining and going off course frustrates and upsets us. That is why we advised writing the first draft of your introduction with no other aim than to find your bearings. A complete revision, consequently, is necessary because much of what you have written will be long-winded ruminations, wordy circlings about, and other manners of false starts. Now is the time to consider capturing your reader's attention with a revised introduction that is both informative and eloquent.

How should you revise your introduction? What should it do? It is only fair that your introduction provide the reader with information that accurately foreshadows the general nature of the essay: you, after all, expect to be able to predict the content of other people's work when you skim their introductory paragraphs. An introduction should genuinely "introduce" what you have to say, "lead" the essay "into" your readers' minds in such a way that they will not feel misinformed once the essay gets underway. Your statement of purpose or thesis may appear in the introductory paragraph, but it alone will not make a good introduction to your essay. Also, your introduction should not reproduce the bluntness of your outline in paragraph form. Be more than merely accurate: try to show your readers something interesting or attractive about your essay so they will anticipate reading it with some pleasure. Following are some suggestions that may help you to revise your introductions:

1. Provide some background information before stating the thesis. This information should not necessarily be used to advance the thesis but should provide an interesting context for it.

2. Raise a question (or series of questions) that your essay will consider, and save the answer for the conclusion. A question may attract the reader more quickly than a declaration. Using a question is not, however, permission to sit on the fence, wander, or otherwise neglect your thesis.

3. State the problem or dilemma that your essay will resolve and the circumstances that led to its emergence. You might summarize the solutions to be considered in your essay.

4. Emphasize the difference between your evidence and that of other researchers, or between your interpretation and someone else's. Such an introduction places your essay in the context of scholarly debate.

5. Use a quotation from either a primary or secondary source. You might choose a passage that captures the main focus of your work. Controversial quotations can kindle the reader's imagination, and ones that you disagree with and disprove can make sparks fly.

6. Anticipate the reader's possible objections to your approach or interpretation and show quickly why they are not valid.

7. Begin with a paradox or apparent contradiction.

8. Begin with a specific example, illustration, or anecdote that is interesting and apt.

9. Define the scope of your investigation. Indicate its parameters and your reasons for choosing them.

10. If you are writing in a discipline such as philosophy or sociology, you may wish to define clearly the way in which you will use particular words, or the way in which you interpret certain words used in the work you are writing about.

Avoid:

1. "The purpose of this essay is to prove that . . . ." In fact, avoid all conspicuously self-conscious announcements of what you have done, are doing, or will do. Usually the sentence survives excision of such nervous words, and is the stronger for it. If the sentence collapses, it did not contain an assertion and needs to be rewritten. Instead of saying, "First I will examine the east and then the west, and finally relate the two together," say, "While it normally rises in the east, the morning sun has been sighted in the west by cattle ranchers in Alberta, and can be shown at times to appear in both horizons simultaneously."

2. Dictionary definitions. These are boring, and rarely help.

3. An opening sentence that echoes the instructor's question or the essay title, or depends upon the title to be understood. Such a sentence indicates a lack of understanding and imagination. Anyone, not just the instructor, should be able to understand your introduction.

4. The inflated declaration of a cliché or a commonplace idea. For example, "Ever since the dawn of mankind people have needed to eat/ engaged in war/ searched for meaning/ loved the simple pleasures."

5. Apologizing for your subject or opinions. Nervous noises such as "In the limited time and space of a term paper . . . ," "As a novice in the discipline . . . ," and so on, should be edited out. If you are feeling nervous, tell your dog. Do not tell your instructor, at least not in your essay.

6. Gratuitous personal preambles. "At first I thought biology was dull, but then I had a great teacher in grade 12, and after doing the research for this essay, I really think I might major in it . . . ." You are tempting your instructor to respond, "Who cares?"

EXERCISE EIGHT: INTRODUCTIONS

Decide which of the following are good introductory paragraphs and which are weak, and give reasons for your answer.

1. (From an essay on John Wilkes)

   In 1763, at the approximate mid-point in his life, John Wilkes joined the cause of liberty. It was an alliance that was to prove beneficial to Wilkes as well as to the cause of which he made himself the symbol. The events from 1763 into the 1770s are ironic in the extreme: a man whose main, perhaps only, motivation was self-interest had the effect of furthering the interests of all men.

2. (From an essay on the Prometheus myth)

   This is an attempt to discuss the Prometheus myth with the aid of pictures and quotations from ancient authors. Sophocles called him "The Lord of Fire." Aeschylus sees Prometheus in the role of fire bringer, as evidenced by the title *Prometheus the Fire Bringer*, one of two lost plays in the Promethean trilogy.

3. (From an essay on Frank Lloyd Wright and Louis Sullivan)

   Louis Sullivan and Frank Lloyd Wright, two important American architects who began to claim the attention of the international architectural community in the late 1800s, both advocated the tenets of "functionalism," the most important architectural movement of the early twentieth century. Because they were contemporaries and both proponents of functionalism, Sullivan and Wright are often looked upon as having made similar contributions to architecture. However, the buildings they designed demonstrate their differing interpretations of the new architectural concept.

4. (From an essay on fantasy and reality in *Who's Afraid of Virginia Woolf?*)

   Richard Schechner, editor of the *Tulane Drama Review*, greeted Edward Albee's *Who's Afraid of Virginia Woolf?* with the charge that it was "a persistent escape into morbid fantasy." But does the play really urge us "to escape reality," as Mr. Schechner maintains? Although the play is certainly concerned with fantasy and reality, fantasy is hardly shown as the more desirable alternative. Indeed, in the final moments of the drama, the characters are brought to a head-on confrontation with reality.

5. (From an essay on utopian and scientific socialists)
   This essay will deal with history. At first, this seems to be a ridiculous statement for a history term paper, but everything that appears to be is not always so.

6. (From an essay on the Progressive movement)
   The Progressive movement represents a radical departure from traditional Canadian politics. The first federal "third party" elected to Parliament, it channelled western agrarian discontent toward Ottawa and made eastern politicians aware of the prairie voice in Canadian politics.

7. (From an essay on *Wuthering Heights*)
   One of the best novels in literature is the novel *Wuthering Heights*. Early in the nineteenth century, author Emily Brontë wrote this brilliant plot. But, as the world turns, so do the critics. One in particular, James Hafley, argues that Nelly Dean is a villain. In my essay I hope to refute Hafley's views.

8. (From an essay on the CCF)
   The CCF Party in Canada had elements in common with the Labour Party in Britain, another socialist party. Socialism is a very broad term, and it encompasses many different ideologies and strategies. In fact, the CCF Party was quite different from the NDP which grew out of it. And of course there are differences between national and regional organizations in the NDP.

9. (From an essay on school closure)
   Declining enrolment in recent years has left many schools half empty, and economic hard times have put school trustees under pressure from taxpayers to reduce the high costs of education. However, the obvious solution — to close schools — is often met with furious protests by parents and neighbourhood groups. Does the closing of schools have the harsh economic and social effects on the community that parents fear? And if so, are there viable alternatives to the problems caused by fewer students and a shrinking dollar?

10. (From an essay on treason)
    Why do people commit treason? By looking at four British spies, Burgess, Maclean, Philby, and Blount, who were recruited for the Soviet Union in the 1930s, I will try to understand why a man might spy against his country. However, I am neither a spy nor British, and so it is possible that I might not really understand the psychology of the spy.

Conclusions

However difficult it is to write and revise an introduction, drawing a piece of prose to an effective conclusion is even more challenging. The chief block to producing a good conclusion is coming to the hard realization that, in finishing something, we are never pretending to have exhausted the topic. An essay, like a life, may be concluded but it can never be complete: there will always be something left undone. Once we acknowledge this fact, the anxiety over the completion of a work can be converted into the pleasure of rhetorical closure, of saying goodbye to the reader in an informative manner. Finishing an essay is not unlike leaving a room or departing a party: you want your audience to remember you and to think and speak well of you when you are gone.

The effective conclusion to an essay stimulates the reader to think more about the topic, and to think about it in a critically open-minded way. While it should return the reader to the larger view of the terrain you have covered, a conclusion should not just reiterate the premise and method set out in the introduction. To "say what you are going to do" in the introduction, to "do it" in the body of the paper, and to "point out that you've done it" in the conclusion is not to write an essay. In fact, a conclusion may well posit a new beginning by suggesting further avenues of pursuit which could not be dealt with because of the formal limitations of the writing.

Although the best conclusions are creative, they also exude a sense of the writer's control. One should "feel" the essay coming to a close, just as one would feel a piece of music resolving the variations upon its theme into one last expression; in this sense, a conclusion is as much a matter of tone as of content, less what one says than how one says it. Following are some suggestions on how to say it:

1. In an essay that has begun with a question, include the answer in the conclusion.

2. Use a significant quotation (probably not from a secondary source) that supports the thesis. This quotation could, but need not, relate to a quotation used in the introduction.

3. Use an anecdote that supports the thesis.

4. If your essay has pointed out a problem or a number of problems, use the last paragraph to suggest solutions. These problems do not have to be solved completely. Complex problems rarely are.

5. Widen the perspective in the concluding paragraph: show how your thesis has implications beyond the immediate scope of the essay. Be careful, however, not to jump tracks into a whole new topic, or to introduce ideas that you ought to have considered in the essay.

Avoid:

1. "In conclusion (or in summary) I have proved that . . . ." The reader's natural response will be "Oh, have you?"

2. Minor details or afterthoughts. Do not be anticlimactic. If you cannot bear to throw out the gems that you could not fit smoothly into the essay, consider using them as supplementary notes.

3. Qualifying remarks.

4. Apologizing for your opinions.

5. Obvious expressions, fan-mail about literature, writers, historical characters. It is admirable to reveal excellence where it exists, but not to rave about it adoringly instead of relating it usefully to your thesis.

While your conclusion should not be a replica of your introduction, presenting the two as a pair can be effective if, in concluding, you go beyond what you have said in the introduction. You might wish to "book-end" your essay with a pair of quotations, or anecdotes, or events, for example, that seem to capture the essence of the way you see the topic. Symmetry provides a satisfying sense of having come full circle, the journey done, and (assuming you have shown the reader something along the way) of having advanced in insight and understanding.

However you decide to end, do not apologize for your inadequacies. In the words of Nellie McClung, early twentieth-century feminist reformer and member of the Alberta legislature, "Never retreat, never explain, never apologize. Get the thing done and let them howl."[8]

---

[8]Nellie McClung, quoted in *New Canadian Quotations*, ed. John Robert Columbo (Edmonton: Hurtig, 1987) 2b.

EXERCISE NINE: CONCLUSIONS

Decide which of the following would make good concluding paragraphs, and try to name the method of conclusion used.

1. (From an essay on the Progressive movement)
    In conclusion, I believe that I have proven that the Progressive movement conveyed western agrarian discontent to Ottawa and made politicians in the east aware of prairie concerns.

2. (From an essay on the use of corporal punishment in schools)
    "Spare the rod and spoil the child": no enlightened educator these days believes in that old adage. The research we have looked at shows clearly that corporal punishment in schools not only arouses great resentment in the child toward school and authority figures but also unwittingly teaches that problems can be solved by the use of physical force. And yet many teachers are loath to ban the strap. What measures could be introduced that would alleviate teachers' fears that the banning of corporal punishment would bring anarchy to the classroom? Administrators could perhaps reduce teachers' anxieties by providing smaller classes so that teachers could give more individual attention to each child; by seeing that teachers are aware of the newer teaching techniques which minimize confrontation; and by making sure that troubled children are seen quickly by guidance counsellors or outside agencies before their problems become acute.

3. (From an essay on John Wilkes)
    Wilkes did not suffer from his alliance with Liberty. Engraved on his coffin are the words,

    > The remains of John Wilkes,
    > a Friend of Liberty.[5]

    Not "Crusader" nor "Champion," simply "Friend." This is a fitting phrase for a man who well knew what a useful friend the cause of Liberty could be.

4. (From an essay on research into cancer)
    Scientists, then, believe that a cure for cancer will come not from goal-oriented research but from basic research into areas not directly related to cancer. Incidentally, much modern knowledge has arisen from basic research, the implications of which the researcher was never aware. Newton invented calculus so that he could mathematically explain the motion of the heavenly bodies. He had no idea that his invention

would enable man to plot the journey of a spaceship to the moon.

5. (From an essay on techniques of characterization in Tolstoy's *War and Peace*)
Tolstoy's *War and Peace* is a very long novel with a great many characters. If Tolstoy had not been able to make the characters stand out from each other and seem real, this book would have been difficult to follow. As it was, the novel was a pleasure to read.

6. (From an essay on chemical pollution in the Walney River)
The effects of the disposal of chemical waste into the Walney River at Barrow are alarming. But Barrow is only a small town of 6,000, with only one large industrial operation. Add to this picture the pollutants that are pouring into rivers from major cities which are a hundred, two hundred, even three hundred times as large as Barrow, and the size and complexity of the regional problems become apparent.

7. (From an essay on the fall of Berlin)
Of course the conclusions I have reached may not be the only conclusions possible. Those who were there fighting, reporting, directing may have understood the fall of Berlin differently. History will never know who is right.

8. (From an essay on the problems of closing schools)
Closing a school that has strong ties with the community it serves can have deleterious economic and social effects on the whole community. To avoid such harmful results, many school boards have managed to keep schools open and yet balance their budgets by trimming all unnecessary expenditures. Most notably, they have cut administrative costs, and they have provided innovative programs which attract particular groups of students (such as adult and foreign students) who would not otherwise attend the school. Trustees should consider their options very carefully before they walk the political tightrope of closing schools.

9. (From an essay on Einstein's place in modern physics)
When Einstein was asked by a reporter why he did not take along a notebook on his afternoon walks so that he could jot down any important ideas he might have, Einstein replied: "Well, you see, I have so few important ideas." Humility was as vital a part of his genius as was the intuition which led him to see which ideas were truly great. Einstein gave to modern physics three very great ideas, and of few scientists can as much be said.

10. (From an essay on Canadian and American relations in the early 1960s) The poor relationship between the Diefenbaker and Kennedy governments of the early 1960s was, as we have seen, caused by complicated political and historical factors. It has just occurred to me that the characters and backgrounds of Mr. Diefenbaker and Mr. Kennedy — one a Baptist, the other a Catholic, one from a modest, the other from a rich and influential background — might have had as much to do with the misunderstandings between the governments as any political cause.

EXERCISE TEN: INTRODUCTIONS AND CONCLUSIONS
Three of the introductory and concluding paragraphs in the previous exercises correspond to each other. Find the pairs and comment on how well or poorly they work together.

EXERCISE ELEVEN: INTRODUCTIONS AND CONCLUSIONS
Read the introductory and concluding paragraphs of the three sample essays. What are the strengths and weaknesses of these paragraphs? Consider these introductions and conclusions in relation to the content of the essay. How could they be improved?

Checklist: Revising Sections

Paragraphs
1. What is the controlling idea of each of your paragraphs?

2. Have you developed these ideas sufficiently?

3. How long are your paragraphs? Are they shorter than three sentences or do they cover two pages?

4. Are there gaps between the ideas expressed at the end of one paragraph and those expressed at the beginning of the one following it?

5. Have you signalled to your reader the relations within and between paragraphs by using transitions?

6. Do all of the quotations used contribute to the meaning and unity of the paragraphs in which you have placed them? Is ever quotation introduced and commented on sufficiently? Have you worked quotations into your prose gracefully?

Introductions and Conclusions
1. Does your introduction give a clear idea of what the essay is about?

2. How long is your introduction? Do you bore your readers with a wordy introduction, or do you fail to capture their interest because your introduction consists of a bald, unappealing statement of purpose or thesis?

3. Does your essay have a forceful, interesting, and obvious conclusion, or does it seem to wither away?

4. Is your conclusion merely a restatement of your introduction and a précis of your paper, or does it show growth?

5. Does your conclusion read more like the introduction to another essay?

Revising Sentences

Many revisions take place at the sentence level. When examining your first draft, consider how to order your words better, whether your words are well chosen, and whether your sentences correspond to grammatical conventions. These three elements — syntax, diction, and grammar — work together to make your sentences coherent.

Revising Syntax

Syntax provides a sentence with a kind of neurological system. It communicates and coordinates the intention behind the expression of the sentence; it enacts and articulates the desires and objectives behind the thought of the writer. When this system breaks down, the sentence loses its balance, becoming uncoordinated, and the development of meaning is paralyzed. During revision, such dysfunctional sentences must be rehabilitated through the proper use of coordination, subordination, and parallel structure.

Coordination and Subordination

The seven coordinating conjunctions (and, but, or, for, nor, so, yet) are used to link ideas of equal value or to add those ideas together. Unfortunately, many students view the coordinating conjunctions as the sole means of linking ideas within sentences, the result being that clauses that were never intended to be equal are often made to appear so. To relate two ideas that are unequal in rank, a writer can employ subordination (from the Latin meaning "placed lower in rank"); the greater variety of relations possible is reflected in the dozens of conjunctions and relative pronouns used to subordinate. Conjunctions such as "when," "where," "because," and "although" illustrate and define the hierarchy of a sentence; they indicate how the subordinate ideas surround and support the principal concept in the sentence. They may introduce elements of time, cause, purpose, or condition — the when, how, why, and if of an idea. In the simplest sense, subordination compels otherwise isolated ideas to interact and thereby reveal their dominant or submissive positions in the sentence. Consider this example:

1. He cooks. She eats.
2. When he cooks, she eats.
3. Because he cooks, she eats.
4. He cooks so that she can eat.
5. Although he cooks, she eats.

In the first instance we know nothing about the relationship between "he" and "she," and we can merely assume that she is eating what he cooks.

Subordination not only immediately relates the two acts but, in the two subsequent examples, gives us respectively a simple temporal or causal basis for the relation of the cooking to the eating. Examples 3, 4, and 5 each begin through subordination to intimate something about the motives and dynamics that connect "he" to "she" as individual personalities. And in example 5, the simple use of "although" suggests a possible injustice or inadequacy in the relationship between these two people: does she eat and get all the advantages of nutrition even though it is he who cooks and does all the preparation? Or does she eat out of sheer politeness or graciousness even though his cooking is not especially good? Through such implications the sentence has become dynamic: its static observations have been transformed into elements that are related.

EXERCISE TWELVE: REVISING SYNTAX THROUGH COORDINATION AND SUBORDINATION

Combine the following sentences using coordinating and subordinating conjunctions as well as relative pronouns. There is a list of these words in Appendix C. Think about the complex sentences you create. Which of these sentences express interesting ideas worthy of further investigation? Write the paragraphs suggested by these sentences.

1. Nuclear power is costly.
   Nuclear power produces potentially deadly wastes.
   We do not yet know how to dispose of these wastes safely.

2. North American Native people suffered from sicknesses.
   They recognized these sicknesses as European.
   They would often accept European remedies.

3. I saw a wild hog foraging in the woods.
   The hog's face was covered with mud.
   It reminded me of my brother eating spaghetti.

4. Car manufacturers spend millions of dollars on research.
   They spend this money to develop small-horsepower engines.
   These engines will travel twice as far on a gallon of gas as today's engines.

5. Scientists must be aware of the advantages of their discoveries.
   They must be equally aware of the disadvantages of their discoveries.
   Their role is difficult.

Parallel Structure

Parallel structure treats two elements of a sentence as equal in rank. The structure is used to list elements or to compare them, and because of the grammatical similarity of the elements, the reader is able to hold them together in mind. Parallelism thus encourages the connecting, building, integrating activity of mind that makes for exciting reading. It enhances writing in the way that analogy does: an effective parallelism will make the reader feel an active part of the intellectual movement of a sentence. All this is due to the symmetrical repetition of phrases and grammatical constructions within parallel units of a sentence. Consider the following example:

> In our primitive past, survival was a physical struggle against famine, war, and pestilence; in our contemporary world, it is an intellectual struggle against apathy, selfishness, and isolation.

Here the structure itself is relatively simple, but the activity of mind it sets up is rich and complex. The parallel structure begins with an opposition of past and present predicates ("was" and "is") across the fulcrum of the semi-colon. The tension extends to semantic contrasts: "primitive" and "contemporary" times, "physical" and "intellectual" struggles. The meaning, however, resides in the association of psychological conditions like "apathy, selfishness, and isolation" with the historic evils of "famine, war, and pestilence." What is a group concern in the first half of the sentence is applied to the individual in the second to evoke an inescapably critical and pessimistic conclusion; the ultimate import of the sentence is thus more implied than stated.

EXERCISE THIRTEEN: REVISING SYNTAX BY EMPLOYING PARALLEL STRUCTURE

Write sentences that parallel those below in structure and in general intent. Use punctuation to relate the sentence you have created to the one given, and see what the resulting sentences imply.

1. Our purpose should be to discover the truth rather than to prove ourselves right.

2. We judge our friends by their words and by their deeds.

3. Punctuation is analogous to musical notation in its function.

4.   We have no right to consume happiness without producing it.

5.   One's will reigns at twenty years of age.

Revising Diction

Diction refers both to a writer's choice of words and to the art of speaking itself. It is useful to remember this dual definition since good writing is close to good spoken English, that is, to English as it is seldom spoken. Your words should invite understanding rather than repel it; they should be natural enough to say aloud without seeming awkward or pretentious. Sentences should not appear to have resulted from a laborious effort to construct a marvel of linguistic engineering through heavy reliance on a dictionary or thesaurus. Neither should they be chatty or slangish, because such language is not precise enough to declare rigorous thought. At times, academic writers need polysyllabic words and complex syntax; a thesis adequately argued entirely in short sentences of five-letter words is probably simplistic and bitty. But understanding writing is difficult enough without allowing language to complicate what it is intended to declare. Readers who have to struggle through difficult diction to excavate the meaning of a sentence are not happy when they find it rattling around like a pea in a drum. When you revise your diction, try to think of getting the right fit between your thought and your words.

Also, try to eliminate redundant words from your first draft. Do not, however, slash too many words. Your sentences should have a rhythmic, flowing quality, and if you carve them down to their bare bones they will read in a choppy, staccato fashion. Worse still, they might not communicate your exact meaning. Be neither lavish nor stingy with your language: use as many words as you need and no more.

Since the twin purposes of writing are to refine and to communicate thought, we should try to choose words accurately. Our words should exactly convey our thoughts. Easy advice to give, but difficult to follow. Every individual's understanding of words is different; two people will probably conjure up two distinct images when they read the word "extremist." To one, an extremist could be a male banker who doesn't wear a suit and tie to work. Another might think any banker or anyone who works extreme. Because of the possibility that they will be misunderstood, writers must revise to eliminate vague words. Keep in mind that general, abstract words, while necessary in essay writing, can be misinterpreted by your reader more readily than specific, concrete words. Upon reading "athlete" you might think of a hockey player, someone else might think of a rower, and another person might think of a cyclist. However, we would probably all think of a great Canadian hockey player if we read "Wayne Gretzky" instead.

Another reason to use concrete words in essays is that they show rather than tell your reader what you mean. Poets and novelists rarely rely on abstract words to convey meaning, yet the concrete words they use often express general emotions or ideas. Philosophers, too, usually flesh out their abstract theories with concrete examples. Often, these examples are more memorable than the universals they illuminate. We recall with ease Plato's discussion of a table while we forget his theory of forms. Remember, then, to revise your writing so that your diction is as specific, concrete, and precise as it can be.

Try also to choose words fairly. As we have seen, all words have connotations as well as denotations. Although the words "agreement" and "deal" both mean or denote "an arrangement," the first has a favourable connotation while the second's connotation can be unfavourable. Most writers use the connotative power of words to make their writing expressive and to give it texture, but words that slant your interpretation of truth should be avoided.

EXERCISE FOURTEEN: REVISING DICTION
Below are five versions of the same idea. These versions all use different sorts of words to communicate this idea. Identify the best passage, explain why you chose it, and tell why you didn't choose the other four.

1. Writing carefully is important. It conveys meaning to the reader. Clear writing helps us to think. Employers consider it important.

2. The written medium is oriented toward a dual goal. First, it must provide input for the user. Second, it must capitalize on the interface between thought and symbol.

3. Clear writing refines our thoughts and enables communication with our readers.

4. It is incumbent on the aspiring writer of serious prose to be cognizant of his responsibility to strive for the utmost clarity of elucidation. Since language is inextricably related to the cognitive faculties, we are capable of cultivating our thinking by rendering our language with ultimate precision.

5. It is important to get close to what you mean when you write. Otherwise, the person who's reading your writing won't understand it. Also, you won't be able to get your own ideas down on paper.

EXERCISE FIFTEEN: REVISING DICTION

Revise the following paragraph, or one that you have written, making each noun and verb as specific and concrete as possible. This revision should eliminate the fuzzy thinking that sneaks into writing when general words are used.

> Macbeth wanted power more than anything else. His wife wanted the same thing. So they were really both the same. She talked him into doing what they did, but really they both wanted to. After they did it, they saw things and didn't talk to each other as much as they used to. Finally, everything came true and Macbeth was killed. Hamlet was the same as them, only he had to talk himself into doing it. King Lear was the same, only he didn't want power; he wanted power back. And Othello has always been a problem. Perhaps Francis Bacon wrote it.

Revising Grammar

Conventional grammar, followed carefully, helps a reader understand your writing. Try to think of it as a series of signals to your reader, as a tool aiding communication rather than as an end in itself. Completing any number of drills or exercises designed to teach grammatical rules is useless if you don't learn to use grammar to express yourself in your own particular way. Therefore, always consider the meaning you want to convey before turning to a grammar text in search of a rule to assist in its conveyance. Grammar check software can help with some of your grammar concerns, but not all. Ultimately, it is up to you, the writer, to decide whether your sentences are both correct and effective.

Most students make only a few grammatical errors, but they make these same errors over and over again. It is difficult, however, to find a constant commonality of error. There are as many different grammatical mistakes that can be made as there are individuals to make them. For this reason, and because of the limits of space, we will not provide you with a complete explanation of the conventions of grammar. Such a task is better left to grammar texts. We propose instead to assist you in the creation of your own checklist, one that will help you catch and revise the grammatical errors you frequently make. Initially, you should compile this checklist by considering the following points in light of a returned essay that has been thoroughly commented on and corrected by one of your instructors. Keep revising your personal checklist, however, for the sorts of grammatical errors you make will change as your knowledge of grammatical conventions expands.

1. ***Has your instructor inserted commas in your text?*** If the answer is yes, try to discern where you generally forget to use commas. Perhaps you neglect to place them after introductory words, phrases, or clauses. The sentences "However she looks to the stars for inspiration" and "Built on the site of Byzantium Constantinople became the capital of the Roman Empire" are desperately in need of commas after their introductory elements. Commas also may be used, however, to surround a phrase or word that interrupts the flow of your sentence. In the preceding sentence, for example, "however" is enclosed by commas because it is interjectory, as is "for example" in this sentence. Do you forget to use commas when listing things? Your sentences should contain commas that separate words, phrases, or clauses listed in a series — as this sentence does.

2. ***Do you ever use semi-colons and colons?*** These punctuation marks are often neglected even though they are invaluable in associating two or more ideas. As we have seen, a semi-colon can communicate complicated meanings when used to form a parallel structure. A colon can effectively introduce what follows it: a single word, a list of words, an independent clause, a quotation, or an example or illustration.

3. ***Do you tend to omit or misplace apostrophes that indicate possession?*** Most students understand that they should write "a dog's breakfast," "Cohen's poem," "women's rights," and "ten cents' worth," but they are frequently confused about how to form the possessive of a tiny word: it. Remembering that *it's* means *it is* and that there is no such word as *its'* will help you write *its* when you mean "its importance" or "its beauty." Since you should not use contractions in formal writing, it should be easy to remember that *it's* does not belong in your essay at all. You then have three possibilities: *its* (for possession), *it is*, or *it has*.

4. ***Has your instructor circled or crossed out exclamation marks or question marks?*** Exclamation marks are supposed to follow only truly emphatic, exclamatory sentences like "The President has pressed the button!" Since these exclamations do not frequent scholarly prose, exclamation marks should rarely, if ever, appear in your essays. Question marks are used to indicate direct questions. "He asked if the ozone layer would disappear altogether" is an indirect question, a statement really, so it would end with a period. "Will you please stop smoking" is a polite request that should also close with a period.

5. ***Has your instructor indicated that sometimes the grammatical units of your sentences do not agree with one another?*** Subjects and verbs should agree in number. Most people do this routinely, but sometimes there is an occasional slip if a sentence's verb is far away from its subject. For example, a writer might have difficulty making the subject and verb agree in the following grammatically correct sentence: "The Prime Minister, along with many other politicians, civil servants, and government appointees, opposes this initiative." A pronoun must also agree in number with the noun it refers to; it must be plural if its antecedent (the noun the pronoun is replacing) is plural, and singular if its antecedent is singular. "Typical students, while concerned about grades, essay deadlines, and imminent exams, have time to explore some of the athletic, social, cultural, and intellectual benefits open to them at university." In this sentence, the antecedent "students" is plural, as is the pronoun "them."

6. ***Are your pronoun references clear?*** If a pronoun's antecedent is remote, ambiguous, vague, or missing, readers will be confused.

   a) *Remote Reference*: Pronouns that are distant from the nouns they refer to often cause readers to search through prose for meaning. In the following passage, the pronoun "it" is too remote from its antecedent "Meningitis."

      Meningitis is an inflammation of the tissue covering the brain and spinal cord. Symptoms include headaches, vomiting, and fever. Sufferers also complain that light hurts their eyes, that they cannot bend their necks without pain, and that they are drowsy. Anyone with these symptoms should see a doctor as it is an uncommon but serious condition.

   b) *Ambiguous Reference*: If a pronoun might refer to more than one noun, its reference is ambiguous. In the sentence "We admired Jane's prize-winning Newfoundland bitch while she went off to find her offspring," the pronouns "she" and "her" could refer either to Jane or to the dog.

   c) *Vague Reference*: Misuse of the pronoun "this" is most likely to cause this error: "Donovan's argument that the American political system dilutes pressures in American society for more economic equality is well founded. This is complicated by the political power of wealthy interest groups." Here, the writer could be referring either to Donovan's argument or to the process whereby pressure for economic equality is diluted.

d) *Missing Antecedent*: A pronoun must refer to a noun. If this noun is only implied, but is nowhere named, then the pronoun is said to be missing its antecedent. "As she watched the sailboat, it suddenly got up, filling the sails." Obviously, the writer means that the wind got up, not the sailboat.

7. ***Has the relation between a modifying word or phrase and the element modified been made clear?*** Misplaced modifiers can create vague or unintentionally humorous sentences: "The minister chatted informally about the cost of living with several women." Presumably, the minister is chatting informally with several women, not chatting about how much it costs to live with several women. Sometimes, a modifier squints, looking both to its left and to its right in search of a word or phrase to modify. In the sentence "Post offices are open on Saturdays only in the country," we don't know whether "only" modifies "on Saturdays" or "in the country." Occasionally, a modifier will dangle unattached to any word in the sentence that is its nominal home. Dangling modifiers are frequently verbal phrases within sentences written using the passive voice: "After lying, stealing, swearing, smoking, playing hooky, and winning a Sunday School prize by fraud, a small fortune in gold is Tom Sawyer's at the end of the story." The small fortune in gold does not lie, steal, swear, smoke, play hooky, or win prizes; Tom does.

8. ***Do your sentences tend to be too exclusive or too inclusive?*** Do you frequently create sentence fragments, fused sentences, or comma splices? No matter how many times "A nice way to start saving for a Steinway" flashes on your television screen, it is still a sentence fragment because it does not contain a subject or a conjugated verb. You are most likely to write a sentence fragment that has both a subject and a verb but that is incomplete because it depends upon another clause for meaning. Neither "But only for charity, never for pay" nor "When I returned in the evening" are sentences. The first is a phrase, without a verb and the second is a subordinating clause, without a main or finite verb. A fused sentence occurs when two sentences or independent clauses are run together without any punctuation between them: "The love of liberty is the love of others the love of power is the love of ourselves." A comma splice creates a similar jamming together of independent clauses even though these two clauses are separated by a comma: "Each dog grows to resemble its owner, that is its tragedy." Comma splices frequently occur because

writers mistakenly believe that conjunctive adverbs such as "consequently," "however," "therefore," and "nevertheless" have the connecting power of conjunctions like "and" and "but." An example of this sort of comma splice follows: "Road repairs may cause traffic jams, nevertheless, some repairs must be made even during heavy traffic."

EXERCISE SIXTEEN: REVISING GRAMMAR
Correct the sentences given as examples of grammatical errors in the section above. There may be more than one answer.

EXERCISE SEVENTEEN: REVISING GRAMMAR
The following paragraph contains examples of some common errors in grammar. There are nine in total. Read the passage aloud to help you identify them all. Then, revise the passage to correct its grammar and to make stylistic and syntactic improvements.

To "sum" an existence, "bound" a life, and find safety in the "strait limits" of an enclosed mind. This must of been the motive of the fictional autobiographers of Charlotte Brontë's novels. Because all three autobiographers seem to need to oversimplify both their own natures and the worlds in which they live in. They are all different, however, they go and do it in basically the same way! Repressing what her more instinctual impulses tell her about the complex truths of experience; this is how they generate personal mythologies by which to rationalize their lives.

Checklist: Revising Sentences

Syntax
1. Are the ideas expressed within each sentence properly linked through coordination or subordination? If you depend too much upon coordinating conjunctions, you might unintentionally be making unequal ideas appear equal.

2. Have you used parallel structure to connect and compare sentence elements and the thoughts they represent?

3. Are your sentences generally balanced and symmetrical?

Diction

1. Have you used language that is clear and easy to understand?

2. Are there any words that have not been adequately defined?

3. Have you avoided slang and jargon? Are the words you use too informal, or have you written in a kind of "bureaucratese" or "computerese"?

4. Is your language as concise as possible? Eliminate deadwood, redundancies, and trite expressions. Don't be self-indulgent. Cut unnecessary words and clever but irrelevant asides.

5. Is your language so sparse and simple that you risk boring your reader? Make sure you have enough words to express your meaning in an interesting way.

6. Have you always attempted to use an exact word to convey your precise meaning?

7. Do your words tend to be general or specific, abstract or concrete? You should usually choose the concrete word unless an abstract word is more accurate.

8. Have you used words fairly?

Grammar

1. Check to see if your grammar is conventional by using the personal checklist you have prepared.

2. Consult previous marked essays to ensure that you don't repeat grammatical errors.

Proofreading

Proofreading is not the same as revising. While revising means looking again at the whole of your first draft and its constituent parts, proofreading implies taking a last look at your almost complete essay. Since "proof" is a publishing term for the typeset version of a writer's text, by the time a writer reads a proof, it is very close to its final version. Proofreading is the writer's last chance to check this text for minor errors before it is sent to the printing press. Proofread thoroughly what you think is your last printing of an essay; avoid proofreading on a computer screen.

A checklist of things to consider while proofreading follows. Watch in particular for errors in formatting and for typos. Again, although a spell check can be of tremendous assistance to you, it cannot solve all spelling problems. It cannot detect homonym mistakes, so if the confusion of "their," "there," and "they're" or "two," "to," and "too" is a problem, you must proofread for these variants.

Checklist: Proofreading[7]

1. **Are your words spelled correctly?** Sometimes there are two or more ways to spell the same word, for example: "centre" and "center." Ensure that you choose one variation and stick to it.

2. **How are numbers expressed in your text?** There are certain conventions to follow here. Usually, numbers that can be expressed in one or two words are written out. However, if the numbers are long, or if you are listing more than one number in a sentence, using numerals is preferable.

3. **Have you indicated which words and phrases in your text are titles?** Quotation marks should be placed around the titles of chapters of books, articles, short stories, and short poems. The titles of other works, such as complete books, journals, plays, and films, should be either underlined or, preferably, printed in italics.

---

[7]*Notes on the Preparation of Essays* provides more detailed information on titles in texts, numbers in texts, and proper methods of quotation and documentation.

4. Have you used the proper form when quoting?

5. Do you cite all of your sources using a standard, acceptable method of documentation, and do you stick to this method consistently throughout your essay?

6. Does your bibliography mention all materials you have used? Does your list of references or works cited include all the works you have cited? All bibliographies, lists of references, or lists of cited works should be arranged according to the conventions of documentation.

7. Does your title page or first page of your essay contain all the information your instructor needs? Usually, the student's name, the course name, the instructor's name, and the paper's submission date should appear with the title on an essay's title page or on the essay's first page in the top left corner. Try also to title your essays creatively. A good title is informative and thematic; it indicates the topic of the paper and something of the thesis as well. Two tantalizing yet informative titles are "Through the Glass Darkly: The Role of Windows in *The Watch that Ends the Night*" and "Taking Liberties: British Imperialism as a Cause of World War I."

EXERCISE EIGHTEEN: PROOFREADING
The following paragraph, which has been checked for spelling and grammar
on the computer, still contains fifteen errors that should have been caught
by a careful proofreader. Try to find them all. It will probably be useful to
read the passage aloud slowly.

"Roughing It in the Bush," Susanna Moodies' witty and moving
book about her experiences in Upper Canada during the 1830s,'
seems too capture the essence of Canadian life. However, were is
not for the storytelling skills off another writer, our beloved
Susanna might never of come to Canada. Susannas' husband Dunbr
filled his book Ten Years in South Africa with so many tales of
danger and mishap that Susanna emphatically refused to
accompany him too so terrifying and dangerous a country. It was
unfortunate for the Moodies that Dunbar wrote so convincingly
they undoubtedly would have faired better their then they did in
Canada.

9 Conclusion

AS A STUDENT, you have probably heard the teachers, parents, and other authority figures in your life lament that the younger generation does not know how to write, and that writing proficiency has declined dramatically since (a) their childhood, (b) the beginning of the twentieth century, or (c) any other convenient date in the not-so-distant past. Do not allow these comments to make you feel inadequate, for the deterioration, if indeed it has taken place, is easily explained. The nature of communication itself has altered in the past several decades. Electronic forms of communication have nearly eliminated the practice of writing letters to be sent through the postal service. Television and videos have certainly reduced the time spent reading for entertainment. And although computer use requires both reading and writing ability, it is a different kind, less sustained and, often, less formal in structure and spelling. It is only natural, therefore, that the emphasis on fluency in other media has caused a decline in the acquisition of writing skills.

Nonetheless, those who lament the loss are justified. Difficult as the act of writing may be in a world where it is but infrequently performed, it is one means of communication that demands intense and committed engagement with a subject. Watching television is a passive pastime — the box supplies a set of words and images, and the audience receives them; one cannot stop for the activity of thinking critically without missing something. Conversation is active, but imprecise; here you always have the opportunity to backtrack, slow down, or question the speaker, but you also risk getting sidetracked. Writing is incisive and exact. To write an effective essay, a student must contemplate a topic, not merely long enough to form an opinion about it, but long enough to consider the other opinions possible, and to defend his or her stance. Such an act is exercise for the mind, and the inability to engage in it is correctly perceived as cause for alarm.

Furthermore, and more immediate to your purpose, at the university level the essay remains the primary medium for communication, precisely because it does engage the mind. Our continuing refrain throughout this book has therefore been to think your way through the essay. By this we mean not only thinking through the particular subject at hand, but also considering the essay as a subject in itself. Being aware of what an essay is, or can be, its principles of development, its voice and audience, takes the mystery out of determining "what the professor wants": not a particular point of view, but a productive method of approach.

Whether it be a first-year paper or a doctoral thesis, your essay is seen as a contribution to the scholarly community, as "new thought" on a particular topic. It is your response to the material contemplated, for it is your perspective — your research, your ideas, your argument — that makes what you are writing "original" and "new." We stress the importance of a thesis to help you keep this notion of a personal contribution in mind; the thesis is the backbone of a paper because it supplies your rationale for writing and, without that rationale, that personal contribution, your essay will be nothing more than a recording of data.

An essay is not just an interaction between writer and subject, however; it is also an interaction between writer and reader. Once you have thought your own way through the subject, you must polish your prose through revision so that the ideas that seem patently obvious to you become as apparent to the reader. We find clarity in written academic work difficult to achieve because we are accustomed to communicating our ideas differently. Much of this book is devoted to making you aware of the structural and contextual properties necessary in essays that we do not find in media such as email or text messaging.

All essays need to be clear, but they cannot be reduced to standard patterns of development. Your main goal in essay writing should be to refine your thinking such that you can convey your ideas clearly to a reader, and if that end is achieved, almost any means is acceptable. Flexibility is the fundamental rule of composition; the moment you begin to think of the essay as a rigid structure, writing becomes difficult. You will have noticed that in our text we blithely ignore many of the traditional notions of formal writing. We use the first and second person. We end our sentences with prepositions, we start them with conjunctions, and we *italicize* occasionally to emphasize words. We compromise the seriousness of our endeavour by making the occasional joke. Stick to the conventions of form when they make meaning more clear (usually they will), and ignore them when you recognize that they will interfere with the force of your argument. Writing essays is not easy, and writing books about writing essays is no piece of cake either. Often, during the composition of this book, we struggled with the difficulties of the sequential form of prose, knowing that the writing process we were describing could not be reduced to a step-by-step procedure. Sometimes you will write an outline after having completed a rough draft. Sometimes a flash of thought will necessitate a change of thesis late in the essay-writing process. The act of writing will make you think about your topic more deeply and will take you in new directions. Permit yourself, therefore, to move freely when you write a paper: go backwards when you reconsider a concept, move sideways if interesting ideas beckon, jump ahead when fleeting insights demand to be recorded. And use our book freely as well. Do not feel that it is necessary to follow our advice from page one onward: concentrate on what you need to know. Let your argument and your audience determine your direction, and you will have made good use of the opportunity the essay provides to think deeply into your subject, and to reveal that thought to your reader.

Appendices

Appendix A
Terms Commonly Used in Essay Topics

Analyze — break something down into parts in order to understand its workings better by exploring relations between the parts or between the parts and the whole

Compare — explore similarities

Contrast — explore differences

Criticize — give a reasoned judgment about the nature of the subject under discussion; might (or might not) involve evaluation of the accuracy or merit of the subject

Define — give a clear meaning of the word or concept, setting out its limits in a given context

Describe — characterize without critical judgment

Discuss — examine an issue critically; sometimes involves responding to a given perspective, (dis)agreeing in whole or in part

Enumerate — list concisely

Evaluate — appraise carefully, looking at strengths and weaknesses, advantages and limitations

Explain — account for, clarify the "how" and "why"

Illustrate — make clear by means of concrete examples or specific instances

Interpret — offer a perspective on a subject

Justify — show grounds for conclusions; present convincing evidence

Outline — arrange the main points and essential supporting points concisely and systematically; omit minor details

Prove — using evidence and logical reasoning, verify a claim or hypothesis

Refute — using evidence and logical reasoning, disprove the statement or claim made

Relate — show connections and associations

Review — survey something, often a book, and comment critically on it

State — express the main point(s) clearly and succinctly

Summarize — present the main points in condensed form, omitting most details, illustrations, and elaborations

Trace — describe, in narrative sequence, the development of an event or instance beginning at a specified point, often the point of origin

Appendix B
Transitional Words and Phrases

1. *Adding Ideas*
   again, also, and, and then, as well as, besides, equally important, finally, first (second, third, etc.), for one thing, further, furthermore, in addition, in the first place, last, likewise, more, moreover, next, nor, similarly, too
2. *Emphazing Ideas*
   above all, after all, equally important, especially, indeed, in fact, in particular, it is true, most important, of course, truly
3. *Illustrating Ideas*
   an illustration of, for example, for instance, in other words, in particular, namely, specifically, such as, that is, thus, to illustrate
4. *Comparing Ideas*
   in the same way, likewise, similarly
5. *Contrasting Ideas*
   and yet, but, but at the same time, conversely, despite, differently, even so, for all that, however, in contrast, in spite of, nevertheless, notwithstanding, on the contrary, on the other hand, or, otherwise, rather, regardless, still, though, unfortunately, yet
6. *Showing Cause and Effect*
   accordingly, as a result, consequently, for that reason, for this purpose, hence, otherwise, so, then, therefore, thereupon, thus, to this end, with this object
7. *Placing Ideas in Time*
   again, already, always, at first, at least, at length, at once, at that time, at the same time, briefly, during this time, earlier, eventually, finally, first (second, third, fourth, etc.), formerly, gradually, immediately, in future, in the meantime, in the past, last, lately, later, meanwhile, next, never, now, once, presently, promptly, recently, shortly, simultaneously, so far, sometimes, soon, subsequently, suddenly, then, thereafter, until now
8. *Summarizing Ideas*
   all in all, altogether, as has been noted, finally, in brief, in conclusion, in other words, in short, in simpler terms, in summary, on the whole, that is, to put it differently, to summarize

Appendix C
Conjunctions and Relative Pronouns

Conjunctions and relative pronouns can help you to establish the connection between clauses within a sentence.

1. *Subordinating Conjunctions*
   Contrasting Ideas
      although, even though, whereas, while
   Showing Cause and Effect
      because, since, so that
   Placing Ideas in Time
      after, as long as, as soon as, before, once, since, until, when, whenever, while
   Establishing Conditions
      assuming that, if, inasmuch as, in case, in order that, insofar as, provided that, so that, to the extent that, unless, whether

2. *Coordinating Conjunctions*
   and, but, for, nor, or, so, yet

3. *Relative Pronouns*
   who, whom, whose, which, that

Appendix D
Sample Essays

The three student essays that follow are examples of writing in the humanities, the social sciences, and the natural sciences. These essays are good, but they are not perfect. You can best learn from them, therefore, by appreciating their strengths but also by considering how they might be improved, as our exercises on them have indicated in the previous chapters. If you have not done the exercises that address these essays, now would be a good time to go back and do them. Again, we thank the authors of these essays for allowing us to print them.

Sample Essay A

The following essay was written for a second-year English Literature course on Shakespeare. It uses the Modern Language Association (MLA) method of parenthetical citation and listing works, which is preferred in English studies especially when the sources consulted are not numerous. Because the essay is dealing with plays, the parenthetical citations are by act, scene, and lines. Only one book is listed at the end because all the essay's references are to that book and no other.

A Midsummer Night's Dream and *Twelfth Night*

[1] There are many similarities between Shakespeare's comedies *A Midsummer Night's Dream* and *Twelfth Night*. Both involve other-world settings, happy romantic endings, and mistaken identities. But they differ in their portrayal of illusion, and they show different relationships of character to it and to its effects. Shakespeare's comparative treatment of the two characters Malvolio and Bottom is a significant locus of these contrasts between the two plays. In *A Midsummer Night's Dream*, Bottom is a uniformly comedic figure. In *Twelfth Night*, on the other hand, Malvolio is both a comic and a tragic figure. These differences derive from differences in character, and they are the reason *Twelfth Night* thwarts illusion, and acquires wistfulness, whereas *A Midsummer Night's Dream* does not.

[2] Both plays are set in illusion. *A Midsummer Night's Dream* includes fairies in its cast and the title suggests a dream-like world of make-believe. In *Twelfth Night*, Shakespeare again uses the title to indicate that Viola's world is different from the everyday world. Twelfth Night is a time when the natural order is reversed, and revelry or the "Lord of Misrule" becomes sovereign. Olivia falls in love with a boy so young his voice is yet to change (1.4.32-33), and Viola and her brother meet and do not recognize

each other until they compare notes about moles on their father's face (5.1.242-43). Both plays exist in very similar imaginary worlds.

[3] Another characteristic shared by both plays is a romantic theme. In both, couples court and eventually end up together on stage at the ending, prepared to marry. This is a familiar format for romantic comedy. Although *A Midsummer Night's Dream* boasts four loving couples and *Twelfth Night* only two, this is obviously not the significant difference between the light-hearted conclusion of the first and the sombre ending of the second. Love and relationships amongst characters are central themes in both plays. Neither play portrays deep and fulfilling relationships. Love is portrayed in both plays as star-struck illusion. Shakespeare suggests that people love witlessly and helplessly. When they are driven to love, it does not really matter on whom their regard falls. In *A Midsummer Night's Dream*, the mere potion from a flower creates love (2.1.169-72). Shakespeare's romantic love does not grow out of friendship or appreciative knowledge of the loved one's traits. Cupid strikes an arrow, and the lovers are instantly smitten. The Duke becomes hunted like a "hart" by his emotions when his "eyes [do] see Olivia first" (1.1.20,24). When Viola speaks her love verses to Olivia she has to ask whether she is addressing the correct person (1.5.170-72). Viola's comment, "Poor lady, she were better love a dream" (2.2.26), sums up the love relationships in both plays. They are blind-eyed infatuations. Surely it is a dark side of comedy that suggests that love is such a shallow emotion that it can be born and killed so easily. But both plays are equally superficial in their depiction of love and neither seems to lose its comedic status on these grounds. In fact the fairy-tale aspect makes the entertainment light-hearted and is a standard comedic convention.

[4] Both plays also involve mistaken identities or mistaken situations. In *A Midsummer Night's Dream*, Demetrius believes he is in love with Helena, and then finds he loves Hermia. A love potion turns him again towards Helena. Lysander loves Hermia, but under the influence of the love potion, changes and loves Helena. A second application of the potion returns his love to Hermia. Likewise in *Twelfth Night*, Viola and Sebastian are mistaken for one another. Olivia cannot tell the difference between Cesario and Sebastian. And Malvolio acts foolishly after mistaking Olivia's love for him.

[5] Equal portions of illusion, romance and mistaken identity are found in both plays. The settings and story lines of the plays seem almost interchangeable. The important difference in impact between the two plays lies in Shakespeare's treatment of Malvolio and Bottom.

[6] The divergence between the hilarity of *A Midsummer Night's Dream* and the melancholy of *Twelfth Night* lies in the characters of Bottom and Malvolio. There are grounds for comparison of these two characters in

that, unlike the other major male characters, they are the men who either do not win their lady or do not win her permanently. Malvolio's aspirations towards Olivia and Bottom's relationship with Titania begin similarly. When Titania first views Bottom, she exclaims, "What angel awakes me from my flow'ry bed?" (3.1.129). A short while later she says, "O, how mine eyes do loathe his visage now!" (4.1.79). He loves — and loses. Similarly, Malvolio believes he has won the heart of Olivia when he receives the bogus letter. Bursting with happiness, he cross-garters his stockings and tries to please her with smiles (3.4). He soon learns his hope was unwarranted. Both men have risen above their station and won the love of a great lady. Both then find themselves rejected. When Bottom loses his lady, he is undisturbed. But Malvolio is disturbed, and he becomes partially a tragic figure. That is the significant difference between *A Midsummer Night's Dream* and *Twelfth Night*.

[7] Bottom considers that it was a dream and carries on with oblivious joviality rather than with shame or regret. He says, "I will get Peter Quince to write a ballet of this dream. It shall be call'd 'Bottom's Dream', because it hath no bottom; and I will sing it . . . ." (4.1.214-17). Shakespeare arranges, by Bottom's attitude, for comedy to continue. The merry illusion is not interrupted as it is in *Twelfth Night*. In fact, Bottom's next activity is to play-act with his comrades. Symbolically, Bottom's participation in the mechanicals' performance reinforces the fact that everything about the play is unreal. Bottom's loss of his lady does not crush him because neither the actions nor emotions in which he is involved are real. No residual harm comes to Bottom. In fact, by the end of the play, he has been surprisingly well received by Theseus and his guests and has every expectation of receiving a pension from the court as a result of his performance for them.

[8] On the other hand, Malvolio does not "spring back" from his rejection by Olivia and his abuse at the hands of the revellers. He does not, like Bottom, believe he has been the victim of a light-hearted jest or dream. His being cast in prison and accused of insanity and his maltreatment by Toby, Aguecheek, Maria, Fabian and Feste torment him. His excessive seriousness and pomposity are a factor in his receiving such treatment, and perhaps also in his inability to take Olivia's rejection more lightly. Nevertheless, the play's perspective changes in connection with Malvolio's predicament; the comedy acquires a tragic element because Malvolio feels pain and humiliation and expresses it vehemently. His words when in jail, "never was man thus wrong'd" and "they have laid me here in hideous darkness" (4.2.28-30), are serious not comedic. Illusion is shattered. On the last page of the play, Malvolio promises, "I'll be reveng'd on the whole pack of you" (5.1.378). Ironically, this occurs while the couples are coming together in the resolution typical to romantic comedy. His battered

176

appearance and poignant speech make sharp contrast to the image of the couples in a "happily-ever-after" ending. Olivia states, "He hath been most notoriously abus'd" (5.1.379). The twelve days of Christmas are over and reality has intruded on illusion.

[9] At the end of *A Midsummer Night's Dream*, Theseus encourages everyone to suspend criticism and join wholeheartedly into the spirit of the mechanics' play (5.1.82-105). Bottom is not a deep thinker and retains his enthusiasm and zest for life throughout. He could have been humiliated and upset by the loss of his Fairy Queen. In this play, feelings are very superficial. No one seems betrayed by any of the wrongs that are done to him or her. Theseus admits at the beginning of *A Midsummer Night's Dream*, "Hippolyta, I woo'd thee with my sword, / And won thy love doing thee injuries" (1.1.16-17). He then claims that he has decided to wed her in a different spirit. How could Hippolyta be expected to return his love under the circumstances? She, however, shows no signs of being upset by his display of force. Why was Titania not furious with Oberon for making a fool of her? It is in order to steal away the young child in her charge that he manipulates her with a love potion (2.1.185). Why does Titania accept his trickery and carry on with such a light heart? There is very little evidence of strong or meaningful emotional reactions amongst any of the characters in *A Midsummer Night's Dream*. No true pain or harsh reality can touch these characters. No harm ever occurs and the world of illusion remains intact. Puck summarizes the play as a "weak and idle theme" which is "no more yielding than a dream" (5.1.427-28).

[10] By its end, *Twelfth Night*, on the other hand, is charged with Malvolio's emotional reaction. At the beginning of the play, Shakespeare writes from the point of view of the revellers, and sport is made of the puritanical and stuffy Malvolio. As the play unfolds, the perspective alters. The world is revealed through Malvolio's eyes despite the fact that his overbearing seriousness is in part responsible for his treatment. The shift in literary point of view in *Twelfth Night* reinforces the impact of Malvolio's emotional despair and frustration. The General Introduction to the *Riverside Shakespeare* states, "Comedy gains its effect through intellectual detachment of the spectator, tragedy through his emotional involvement" (22). *Twelfth Night* proves the accuracy of this statement. Shakespeare's manipulation of point of view is clearly intentional. Orsino says, "One face, one voice, one habit, and two persons, / A natural perspective, that is and is not!" (5.1.216-17). Cesario is one face but actually two different people: Viola and Sebastian. It is Shakespeare's intent to portray two faces of Malvolio as well, and by including the word "perspective," he underlines this for his readers. By the end, Malvolio's role has changed from that of antagonist of the play's merry world to protagonist in his misfortune. By

changing the point of view, Shakespeare displays the two faces of Malvolio, and the play turns tragicomic.

[11] *A Midsummer Night's Dream* ends in a manner typical of conventional comedy. Problems of mistaken identity have been resolved, love reigns, and a happy ending is to be shared by everyone, including Bottom. Malvolio, on the other hand, is upset, betrayed, and has no "happy-ever-after" ending in sight. The significant difference between the two plays lies in Bottom's acceptance of the attitudes and actions of the people around him and Malvolio's rejection of and by the people around him. Bottom's world remains a happy world of illusion. Reality and emotion invade *Twelfth Night* to incorporate melancholy.

Works Cited

Shakespeare, William. *A Midsummer Night's Dream. The Riverside Shakespeare*. Boston: Houghton Mifflin Company, 1997. 256-80.

---. *Twelfth Night. The Riverside Shakespeare*. Boston: Houghton Mifflin Company, 1997. 442-74.

Sample Essay B

The following essay was written for a second-year course in International Development Studies (IDS). It uses the American Psychological Association (APA) method of parenthetical citation and listing references, which is preferred by IDS. The use of subheadings is acceptable in IDS.

Development, Democracy and Human Rights
Mutually Reinforcing or a Cover for Disempowering Market Reform?

Introduction

[1] Democracy, development, and human rights and freedoms have over the past decade become a triumvirate within the development community. The Vienna Declaration (from the 1993 World Conference on Human Rights) takes the general position that the components of this powerful conceptual triad depend on and reinforce each other (Donnelly, 1999). More conservative views, including the Washington Consensus, champion specifically a combination of international open market capitalism and domestic liberal democracy as essential in creating a "virtuous cycle of development." Such a combination can result in neglect of problems of inequality in development, just as, in its way, the principle of good governance can safeguard basic freedoms but overlook socio-economic inequalities (Potter, 2000).

[2] The Vienna Declaration and the Washington Consensus offer just two examples from the spectrum of ideas in current theoretical discourse on the importance of democracy in development. Since the late-1980s change in global political structures, at the end of the Cold War, development theorizing has moved away from a strictly economic, growth-based approach and toward a human-rights-based focus. A general espousal of the liberal form of democracy — the system presumed to have won the Cold War — as a humanitarian and egalitarian agent of development has contributed to the current seemingly indispensable combination of development, democracy, and human rights. Although all sides seem to agree on and to follow this new triad, there are very different interpretations of each of its components and therefore of the precise configuration of the triad itself. These contrasting interpretations have resulted in a discrepancy among developmental agendas. For, as much as they can be mutually reinforcing, "democracy, development and human rights can also be pursued in ways that are mutually limiting to one another" (Donnelly, 1999, p. 610). Examining these contrasting interpretations of the triad helps us to clarify matters and to highlight the triad's true humanitarian potential, as this potential can be seen in isolated cases such as that of Porto Alegre, Brazil, which is a clear example of a genuine virtuous cycle of economically and humanly sustainable development.

Liberal Democracy, Participatory Democracy, and the Concept of Human Rights

[3] In itself, the principle of democracy holds great promise for supporting long-term economic development that includes improved human rights. The general principle of democracy can risk becoming a cover for policies that rely on an idea of good governance that ignores socio- economic inequities. Such a risk is possible because the traditional, liberal conception of democracy understands freedom as basic political freedom under the law and does not include in the idea of freedom itself an expansion of socio-economic opportunity for the underprivileged. This restriction in the idea of freedom leaves room for the triad of development, democracy, and human rights to be twisted into a triad of political ideals that is able to appease the majority and serve the market without playing its true humanitarian role, as we shall see when we come to the discussion of the effects of neo-liberal economics on democracy.

[4] As a general ideal, democracy always implies, indeed relies for its legitimacy on, the assumption that people are a very important part of its definition and practice, as people are meant to "use their will to control their own political, economic, social and cultural systems" (Vienna Declaration, 1995). A democracy, then, should be an egalitarian system of rule with equal opportunities for citizens to be elected. Yet "democracy" is a very flexible term that embodies a universal, basic set of values in theory that in practice becomes a heterogeneous mixture of different adaptations and interpretations. And the classic liberal model of democracy, because of its emphasis on basic freedoms, as opposed to instituting political processes designed to expand socio-economic opportunity for the underprivileged, lends itself all too well to relative passivity regarding equal opportunities for citizens to be elected.

[5] Participatory governance is one model of democracy that emphasizes values that include human rights and freedoms but also uses a "devolution of decision-making power to the general public" to guarantee fairness and efficiency within the deliberative framework of democracy (Fung & Wright, 2003, p. 46). This form of democracy places responsibility on institutional design, one that is driven by the enhanced participation of the general public, to bring the real world closer to the ideals of democracy. In the case of Porto Alegre, Brazil, the system of "neighbourhood deliberation" was instituted by the ruling Partido dos Trabalhadores (PT) to create a context in which citizens can act and be treated as responsible equals to those who govern (Fung & Wright, 2003). Human rights for an empowered participatory democracy are seen to be such an integral part of the functioning of the democratic structures that they are placed on a level of importance equal to that of the democratic process itself, thus maintaining one important link between two major factors in the triad of

development thought. "An inalienable set of individual goods, services and opportunities," human rights and freedoms are generally the responsibility of the state and society to respect and to provide (Donnelly, 1999, p. 620). But the PT has approached this challenge in a unique manner. Through an apparent inversion of what results from traditional liberal-democratic practices, popular participation and the use of a participatory budget have created an increased focus on the poor and marginalized sectors of Porto Alegre. A socio-economic range of citizens allocate funding and monitor projects in the participatory budgeting system. The results have been an increase in access to basic amenities and an increase in monetary support for housing assistance and schools (Fung & Wright, 2003). Porto Alegre also provides a perfect illustration of Amartya Sen's concept of development as freedom (1999). In providing direct means of "political freedom" to criticize and contribute to the functioning of the government, the PT has created a democratic environment in which other social opportunities, such as education, have been enhanced, and the right to protective security has been ensured by an improved safety net, as, for example, in housing assistance. In this way the PT has encouraged genuine human development.

Defining Development

[6] In general, development is a process of growth, change, or activation; whether one is enhancing an economy or a person, development can be seen as a process toward improvement. Sen's humanitarian definition of development portrays the process as an expansion of the "real freedoms" of the individual through improvements in social, economic, political, and civil rights (1999, p. 5). These freedoms act as a means for creating yet greater freedom (Sen, 1999). In this view, sustainable development is a process "of the people, for the people, by the people" (Kyi, 1995, p. 14). In support of an idea of the components of the triad as mutually reinforcing, Kyi argues that "democracy is the political system through which an empowerment of the people occurs for sustained human development" (1995, p. 16). This human-rights definition of development is important; however, it is the narrowly socio-economic concept of development that is currently receiving more attention from the mainstream development think tanks.

[7] For this more conservative bloc, development is defined as improvement in terms of aggregate growth (increase in Gross Domestic Product, GDP) or increases in industrialization (Donnelly, 1999). There is a general consensus among neo-liberal thinkers that the greater the GDP of a country, the more improved the standard of living for all of the inhabitants of this country. Such thinking does not take into account inter-group contrasts and inequalities. As Sen (1999) points out, an often

underprivileged minority in the United States, the African Americans, "have an absolutely lower chance of reaching mature ages than do people of many third-world nations" who are all equally poor (p. 6). Markets foster commercial effectiveness but not social justice or the equal enjoyment of individual rights for all. Efficient markets improve the lot of some, at the relative cost of suffering by others even if the suffering is an invisible burden like lowered life expectancy (Donnelly, 1999).

[8] The 1993 United Nations Human Development Report suggests that "both state and market should be guided by the people, and people should be sufficiently empowered to exert effective control over both" (Kyi, 1995, p. 17). Such empowerment does not come from increased aggregate wealth, as suggested by the neo-liberal dogma, but by increased equity and human rights. In much the same way that democracy in its sheer sense of majority rule is championed, this dogma justifies free markets by arguments of the collective good and aggregate benefits, not the rights of the individual (Sandbrook, 2002). The neo-liberal standard of development sees growth of wealth and material gains as the "primary end" of development and as a result of this notion a disproportionate amount of attention is placed on the market. And the reality is that quite often a regime's ability to foster development in the form of economic prosperity for the majority will create legitimacy for the regime amongst the greater population.

Neo-liberal Economics and the Principle of Democracy

[9] As defined by the World Bank, democracy is "a means in which power is exercised in the management of a country's economic and social resources for development" (Potter, 2000, p. 370). In conventional liberal politics, the role of democracy is understood as preventing tyranny and improving governance, not empowering the poor to press governments for favourable policy changes. Relying on this traditional conceptual foundation, the current neo-liberal economics of institutions like the World Bank construes the management of a country's economic and social resources for development in a manner that makes market freedom synonymous with political freedom. As Polanyi (2001) argues, however, "to allow the market mechanism to be sole director of the fate of human beings and their natural environment would result in the demolition of society" (p. 73). But even if such a drastic outcome were not to occur as a result of the increased uncoupling of the market and the spirit of community, such separation would result in conflicts between the market's energies and the impetus for improvements in social, economic, political, and civil rights, that is, the real freedoms of the individual, as defined by Sen.

[10] Neo-liberal economic ideology often views growing inequalities as a regrettable by-product of expanding productivity or as a welcome recognition of different levels of contribution to productivity (Sandbrook, 2002). Thus, the role of democracy in a neo-liberal capitalist country is often limited to low-intensity regulatory organization that ensures the freedom of the market and prudent macroeconomic policy. Such organization ensures minimal safety nets and services for those who "fall through the cracks" of the market system, consequently forestalling backlash against neo-liberal economic practices and promoting complacency regarding government policies.

[11] The neo-liberal economic view, therefore, is creating situations in which "democratization is becoming synonymous with destatisation," as governments slowly attempt to release the market from society (Abrahamsen, 2000, p.53). Consequently, good governance, in itself a valuable principle of civil society, ends up supporting unbridled free-market economics and sustaining sound-management principles of the kind that privatizes production and encourages market-led growth by enforcing rules that create a stable environment for investment (Potter, 2000). In development, these ideas have been embodied in the structural adjustment programs (SAPs) prescribed by the World Bank and other prominent organizations, like the International Monetary Fund (IMF). In response to the purported failure of state-led industrialization, such prescription relies on the abridged, weakened idea of good governance just indicated to provide the link between democracy and economic development. Yet, despite such a limited idea, this prescription still manages to claim cultural awareness because of its espousal of a rather broad notion of democracy as an institution "of the people, by the people, for the people."

[12] In fact, however, neo-liberal economics leads to a politics that is tantamount to an excuse for democracy, and it is about as culturally sensitive as modern free trade and capitalism are attuned to indigenous cultures in countries that exchanged goods along caravan routes (Abrahamsen, 2000). What is called good governance assists in the gradual weakening of the state and opening of the market to increased foreign investment and trade in the developing world. Instead of encouraging the state to protect human rights, the increased competition for larger shares of the market and increased investment has led to the proverbial race to the regulatory bottom, as states shed or lower standards of enforced labour rights and protective laws.

[13] The link between development and democracy, therefore, becomes quite thin, and their relative importance to one another exceedingly uneven. With such a back-burner role for true, people-empowering democracy and goals for development, even basic human rights, it would seem, could be lost or reduced as well. The reason is that "human rights" has become

a rather loose phrase built into varied definitions of democracy. Donnelly (1999) argues that human rights and the institutions that uphold them are in fact quite anti-democratic when democracy is defined merely as the people's will. For such a glib definition of democracy makes democracy a champion of an aggregate benefit and not an empowerment of individuals. Institutions, such as the justice system, exist, often created by elected governments, but are regularly used to make decisions that are, arguably, undemocratic because they do not reflect the will of the majority. Governments, even those adopting neo-liberal economic ideology, do enforce the protection of some basic human rights. But such protection, though genuine, does not amount to the deeper enhancement of individual choice that the phrase "human rights" may project. (And we mustn't forget that such protection also functions as a minimum legitimization of the ruling power.)

[14] In this way, human rights are required as a force that makes both democracy and markets more humane, but their effectiveness is limited to a domain defined by no more than basic rights and freedoms (Donnelly, 1999). The maintenance of this limited domain provides many liberal democratic states with their hegemonic appeal and prevents the unmitigated domination — and demolition — of society by the market. As for development within this limited domain, quite often equitable distribution will be sacrificed for an increase in capital accumulation and growth; this is known as the equity trade-off (Donnelly, 1999).

[15] On the other hand, when, depending on the country, neo-liberal economics is disconnected from the legislated minimal human-rights requirement that characterizes liberal-democratic countries, the equity trade-off can go hand in hand with a liberty trade-off, whereby civil and political rights are sacrificed in the name of efficiency or concerted effort (Sandbrook, 2002). When this occurs, as in non-liberal-democratic states, the combination leads to authoritarian and totalitarian political regimes under which very few rights exist. In this scenario, what we get is the antithesis of everything that the mutually reinforcing triad of development, democracy and human rights is meant to suggest. Thus have the newly industrialized countries (NICs) of south-east Asia developed economically and flourished using rights-restricting tactics. They seem to have proven that discipline is more important than democracy, at least for economic development.

[16] Studies have shown that overall economic success or failure is very much a lottery, luck-of-the-draw situation that depends upon a wide range of factors, none of which is directly affected by the prevalent form of leadership found in a country. Governments, whether dictatorships or liberal democracies, were found to be equal on the likelihood of successful economic-growth generation (Potter, 2000). Therefore all such

developmental successes should perhaps be described strictly as economic miracles.

Conclusion

[17] It seems that all economic development is becoming increasingly based on achievements strictly in the aggregate economy, with the market becoming progressively disembedded from society, owing to the advent of free trade and growing globalization. Thinking that conceives development as highly linked with democracy and human rights that are understood to involve the expansion of socio-economic opportunity for the underprivileged, then, offers a clear alternative path for the future. Porto Alegre in Brazil and other revolutionary examples of participatory democracy should move into the forefront of development practice, as the apparent problems with neo-liberal development objectives are becoming increasingly evident. For the future of development, a much higher priority should be placed on political objectives that support human development and Sen's ideas of development as freedom. Participatory democracies, as exemplified by Porto Alegre, should become the newest mainstream means for a development focused on humanitarian principles of protected freedoms, equity, and rights for all. Sen supports the true triadic approach to development, that which champions democracy as the greatest protector of rights, but the current popularity of the mere good governance form of democracy seems to be leading democracy away from being a champion of anything more than basic freedoms.

[18] The supposed virtuous cycle of democracy and neo-liberal economics may promote growth, but, contrary to popular theory, this growth is not improving the situation of unequal rights and unfreedoms that persists around the world. For the future, participatory democracy is worth pursuing as part of the triad of development. Meanwhile, continued discussion and theorizing on democracy and development is necessary for the protection of human rights. Unless democracy and development are pursued in the correct fashion suggested, human rights as anything more than basic legal freedoms are at risk of being forgotten. The slow erosion of human rights has been observed as a current political trend in many states; therefore empowering people to become politically active is one of the most important steps to advancing human rights, the most fragile and easily forgotten of the triumvirate. Theoretically, one cannot always tell whether economic development would lead or not lead to a deepening of democracy, or vice versa. But, with a strong respect at the helm for human rights as something more than mere basic legal freedoms, a triumvirate of democracy, development, and human rights can be the most important strategy for economically and humanly sustainable development.

References

Abrahamsen, R. (2000). *Disciplining Democracy: Development Discourse and Good Governance in Africa.* London: Zed Books.

Donnelly, J. (1999). Human rights, democracy and development. *Human Rights Quarterly*, 2(3), 608-632.

Fung, A., & E.O. Wright (2003). *Deepening Democracy: Institutional Innovations in Empowered Participatory Governance.* London: Verso.

Kyi, A.S.S. (1995). Freedom, development, and human worth. *Journal of Democracy*, 6(2), 11-19.

Polanyi, K. (2001). *The Great Transformation.* Boston: Beacon Press.

Potter, D. (2000). Democratization, "good governance" and development. In T. Allen & A. Thomas (Eds.), *Poverty and Development: Into the 21st Century* (pp. 365-379). Oxford: Oxford University Press.

Sandbrook, R. (2002). Deepening democracy to fight poverty. *International Journal*, 57(2), 175-192.

Sen, A. (1999). *Development as Freedom.* New York: Random House.

Vienna Declaration. (1995). Office of the High Commissioner for Human Rights, Geneva. Retrieved on Nov. 18, 2003, from the World Wide Web: http://www.unhchr.ch

Sample Essay C

The following essay was written for an upper-year course in biology. It uses a variant of the American Psychological Association (APA) method of parenthetical citation and listing references; such a variant is sometimes used in biological studies. The use of subheadings is acceptable in biological studies.

Habitable Planets
Just Beyond Our Reach

Introduction

[1] A fundamental question pondered by evolutionists concerns the existence of life on Earth and our place in the Universe: are we alone? This question has been approached from many different viewpoints ever since the revolutionary heliocentric Universe theory proposed by Nicolaus Copernicus moved the Earth from the centre of the Universe and Galileo Galilei converted the Sun into an ordinary star (Hawking 1988). Many considerations make it difficult for evolutionists to agree that the organisms on the planet Earth are the only forms of living material in the Universe, considerations such as the immensity of the Universe, the manner of its creation, the way living material evolved in it from molecules, and the illimitable matter that has not yet been described. In addition, the technology of today permits scientists to study farther planets and stars, and has delivered vast knowledge that supports theories concerning the possibility of extraterrestrial life. Greater knowledge concerning the Universe and planetary systems such as extrasolar planets intensifies the desire to discover habitable planets. More advanced technology is needed, however, to prove the theory that there is life on other planets, and it is the lack of such technology that limits us in our quest to make new discoveries about our Universe.

Origin of the Universe

[2] In order to comprehend the magnitude and complexity of the Universe, we must understand how the Universe was created and the processes that were involved. The most widely accepted theory of the origin of the Universe is known as the Big Bang Theory, expounded by Sir Fred Hoyle in the 1940s. This theory assumes that the Universe is described by a Friedmann model, and supposes that, as the Universe expanded, any matter or radiation in it became cooler. At the point of the Big Bang, 15 billion years ago, the Universe was thought to have zero size, and so to have been infinitely hot; one second after the Big Bang, however, the Universe had cooled to about ten thousand million degrees and contained mainly photons,

electrons, and neutrons. At one hundred seconds, the temperature fell to one thousand million degrees, at which elements such as deuterium and helium were created. The formation of these elements was crucial, as they gave rise to heavier elements such as lithium, beryllium, and eventually hydrogen (Hawking 1988). After 1 billion years, the temperature was 20K, and galaxies and stars began to form via gravitational contraction of overdensities in the initial Universe. Nuclear-fusion reactions of stars converted helium into heavier elements that in turn resulted in the production of carbon and oxygen. These heavier elements had been blown back in tremendous explosions referred to as supernovas that provided some of the raw material for second-generation stars (Stebbins 1969). A few billion years later, our galaxy formed, and at about 10 billion years after the Big Bang, the Sun and Earth formed. After 15 billion years we reach the present and a background temperature of about 3K (Ducrocq 1956).

Envisioning the Immensity
[3] Having established a general understanding of how the Universe was created, and a relative time scale of the events that took place leading to the creation of our Sun and solar system, we should examine the size of the Universe and the space between the structures within it. According to Ovenden (1962), to obtain the simplest understanding of the magnitude of the Universe one must imagine the Earth being shrunk to the size of a pinhead then envision the Sun 15 metres from the Earth and the size of a 15-centimetre sphere. Jupiter would be the size of a large pea 76 metres from the Sun, and Pluto, the most distant planet, would be a speck of dust over 1.7 kilometres from the Sun. On this same scale, the nearest star would be another 15-centimetre sphere 3200 kilometres from the Sun. As for the size of our solar system in relation to our galaxy, we can consult Ovenden's model and suppose that the galaxy is shrunk to the size of Earth at present. The sun now would be the size of a speck of dust about a fifteenth of a millimetre across, and the stars would be separated by approximately half a kilometre. We should also note that our Sun is just a single star among tens of millions of stars in our galaxy and that our galaxy is but a single one among hundreds of millions present in the Universe.

[4] The immensity of the Universe leads many to believe that it is unreasonable to assume Earth is the sole planet in the Universe that contains sustainable life. Yet this immensity is what prohibits us from reaching possibly habitable planets with our current technology. When we measure distances to them, we find that they are so far away that their light takes years to reach us (Liebert and Hubbard 1999). The nearest star system to our own, called *Alpha Centauri*, is around four light years away (U of Michigan 2003), whereas the nearest galaxy to ours is 2.2 million light

years away. Therefore it is not easy to detect other planetary systems with current telescopes.

Sustainable Existence

[5] What circumstances or sequences are crucial for life to exist? A possible answer to this question was established at an international symposium on the origin of life on Earth held in Moscow in 1957, where forty specialists, including Melvin Calvin, Linus Pauling, and Wendell M. Stanley, determined the five steps necessary for the transformation of inanimate matter into living cells. Their results were as follows (Sullivan 1966):

1. The formation of the simplest organic compounds.
2. The transformation of these simple compounds into more complex organic compounds.
3. The origin of the key life chemicals, such as proteins and nucleic acids.
4. The origin of structures and metabolism (energy-producing chemistry).
5. The evolution of metabolism.

[6] The primary requirements for sustaining life on a planet were further described by Kasting et al. in 1993 as follows: the occurrence of liquid surface and closely related temperature regimes that produce both hot greenhouse atmospheres and carbon-dioxide clouds that reduce the temperature below the aqueous freezing point (Kasting et al. 1993). We also know that the transition from RNA to DNA is an important step toward evolving life (Berrill 2003). Unfortunately, however, current studies that are attempting to recreate the evolution of simple cells, otherwise known as protocells, provide us with an example of how technology limits us. So far, it has been possible to create cells that replicate on their own, yet they do not carry any information (Berrill 2003).

[7] The presence of these requirements of sustainable life then enables the formation of living organisms from non-living matter; the processes involved in this formation may be understood by examining their occurrence on the only planet recognized to sustain living matter: Earth.

Abode for Life

[8] What was it that allowed the Earth to evolve into the vast system of biomass that it is at present, and what processes were involved in the evolution of living matter? Using technology to make discoveries regarding Earth's evolutionary past, and how species on Earth came to be, will lead to explanations that will in turn elucidate how life in distant galaxies may exist (Moffat and Shneour 1986). Initially, Earth was exceptionally hot

and contained no atmosphere and consequently no liquid water and no gases (CIAR 1987). The planet's atmosphere was formed eventually by gas emissions from cooling rock (Lewis and Prinn 1984), but this atmosphere was not fit for the survival of living organisms until Earth cooled to the point where more complex molecules developed in the form of water, ammonia, and methane. The forming of these molecules seems to have resulted from chance combinations of atoms (Hawking 1988). These chance combinations continued and began the process of evolution by the creation and destruction of macromolecules, in a manner somewhat resembling natural selection, until more fit macromolecules originated the development and reproduction of more complex organic structures (Moffat and Shneour 1986). The most essential complex organic structure that arose to allow sustainable life on Earth seems to have been the protein. Organisms need proteins in order to carry out tasks from the most simple to the most complex (Ducrocq 1956). With no proteins in the form of enzymes to catalyze chemical reactions, life would proceed at a sluggish pace, if at all (Sullivan 1966). It is therefore imperative that we ask how proteins are constructed and what elements are required for them to exist. Proteins are composed of chains of amino acids, amino acids are constructed from nucleic acids, and nucleic acids make up the building blocks of life: DNA (Sagan and Shklovskii 1966). Having said that, it is important to indicate that the four most abundant and chemically active elements in the Universe are hydrogen, oxygen, carbon, and nitrogen. And, incidentally, these are also the four prime elements that are vital to the design of the acids just mentioned.

[9] Although protein molecules are essential to life, their existence would not be possible if it were not for the more obvious, measurable constituents enabling sustainable life on Earth. There are many of these, but two stand out: liquid water and the presence of a star that, like our Sun, emits solar light and heat that allow sustainable life. All the Earth's energies are derived from the Sun (Ovenden 1962). Without the Sun, there would be neither light nor heat, and therefore no life in the forms present on planet Earth could exist. Yet it is worth mentioning that until recently it was believed that the range of temperatures living matter could tolerate, with some deviation, is from a few degrees below $0°$ C (freezing point of water) to about $60°$ C (Kasting et al. 1993), and that anything above or below these temperatures would not allow life to continue (Ovenden 1962). But discoveries of archaebacteria in thermal heat vents have proved this assumption untrue. These bacteria are able to live in water temperatures as high as $100°$ C (Gupta 1998). And they are non-photosynthetic; that is, they live without the Sun. Such a discovery suggests that life may exist in forms previously unknown to us, and we need to take this possibility into account when considering the viability of extraterrestrial life. The Sun,

though, is still essential for sustaining other life forms, such as chemicals required by non-photosynthetic organisms (Gupta 1998).

Importance of Lower-Mass Stars

[10] Given that the Sun provides the Earth with energy to perform life-sustaining tasks, a star like it must be present in order to supply a planet with energy. So the question now is, what stars are most likely to enable habitable planets?

[11] To support life, a planet must have water on its surface for a long time, and for this it needs a lower-mass star much like our Sun. That is how continuously habitable zones come to exist. When the planet is in orbit, these zones are exposed and may maintain liquid water on their surfaces for billions of years (Wetherill 1995). High-mass stars will not serve such a life-sustaining purpose. They are much hotter than lower-mass stars and use up their fuel far more rapidly, so that, even if Earth-like planets form around high-mass stars at distances where liquid water is stable, it is unlikely that benign conditions would exist long enough on these planets to enable life to form and evolve. Life would only be possible if a greater flux of ultraviolet radiation sped up biological evolution enough to compensate for the shorter lifetime of a massive star (Lissauer 1999). At the other end of the size spectrum, the lowest-mass stars can live for trillions of years, but they emit almost all of their luminosity at infrared wavelengths and cannot support a system as complex as that of Earth. In addition, habitable-zone planets orbit so close to these faint stars that their rotation is tidally synchronized, much like the moon in relation to the Earth (Kasting et al. 1993). Therefore no day-night cycle occurs, and if the planet's atmosphere is thin, it would freeze on the dark, cold hemisphere.

[12] In the last decade before the millennium, discoveries were made of more than 20 planets in orbit about stars other than our Sun (Hughues 1998). These planets are referred to as extrasolar planets; their discovery is crucial to understanding how the Universe operates. And with the proper technology, evidence of planets orbiting lower-mass stars may eventually lead us to habitable planets.

Extrasolar Planets

[13] Scientists have speculated that there were systems much like ours yet to be discovered in the Universe. In particular, James F. Kasting thought that these systems may be identified using an interferometer/spectrometer and a well-developed absorption feature to detect levels of oxygen (Kasting 1996, 1997). Though scientists did not know when such a discovery would be made, they acknowledged that, if made, it would provide further support for the possibility of life on planets other than Earth.

[14] The first discovery of an extrasolar planet was made by Michel Mayor and Didier Queloz of the planet orbiting 51 Pegasi (Marcy 1998). Its discovery suggested that not all anticipated arrangements in the Universe were necessarily based on what had been observed or predicted. This was because the planet identified exhibited an orbital period of 4.2 days, which implied that it was 20 times closer to its star than the Earth is to our Sun (Marcy 1998). And the mass of the planet was half that of Jupiter's, though it was a mere 0.05, rather than the expected 5, astronomical units from the star's surface (Hughues 1998). In other words, an orbit with such a close proximity to the star was previously unimaginable.

[15] Other discovered extrasolar planets, found around Rho Cancri A, Tau Boötes A, Upsilon Andromedae, and Rho Coronae Borealis (Hughues 1998) have been something of a disappointment to those in search of extraterrestrial life because they did not resemble anything similar to the one we inhabit. However, one extrasolar planet discovered around 47 Ursae Majoris brought some hope, for this planet had more closely related attributes to those in our solar system, such as its mass and orbiting manner (Marcy 1998).

[16] The reality is that we have not yet come across a planet that has shown evidence of sustainable life, nor a possibility of future life. But we do have a foot in the door, so to speak, because of discoveries of planets with "Suns." And by studying these planets and their stars we will learn more about their components and thus make predictions concerning similar structures. At present, we know little about each one; however, their discovery will lead us to information that was unattainable before knowledge of their presence.

Current and Future Studies

[17] Recent progress in cosmology and astronomy has been remarkable. For example, it was only in the third decade of the last century that galaxies were proven to be separate bodies of billions of stars distributed across vast amounts of space, not, as many thought, gaseous nebulae inside our own galaxy (U of Michigan 2003). Today, using the high-resolution capabilities of the Hubble Space Telescope (HST) and the large light-gathering abilities of 8-metre-class to 10-metre-class ground-based telescopes, we routinely detect galaxies that are observed when the Universe was only 5% to 10% of its present age (Hamilton 2001).

[18] According to an online website regarding the technologies used to detect extraterrestrial life, the National Research Council (NRC) has released a report that reviews techniques and technologies for detecting past and present extraterrestrial life (Astrobiology 2002). Complicating matters, however, is the fact that astrobiologists don't yet agree over what

constitutes evidence of life. The most sensitive equipment for detecting life in the laboratory is too cumbersome to lug to other planets. The report therefore recommends that researchers press ahead with the miniaturization of life-detection technologies. Returning samples to Earth would make possible a wide array of analyses in the laboratory. But it is a technically daunting proposition because scientists believe that, even if an organism is detected, it could be an Earth organism that was carried along on the spacecraft. Therefore it is essential that the spacecraft be sterilized to the fullest extent practical before launch. Yet sterilization by heating the spacecraft could damage flight hardware.

[19] The prospects of finding many more extrasolar planets are good because of the growing interest of scientists in the field and the advance in technology within the past decade. Feats that once seemed entirely impossible, such as observing planets in other galaxies, are now well underway. Furthermore, studies in recent years, in which microbiologists made startling discoveries about the hardiness of life on Earth by studying living organisms in thermal vents, acid lakes, and other unlikely environments have paved the way for new research. Dr. Kenneth Nealson, a scientist at NASA's Jet Propulsion Laboratory, points out, "This has opened the eyes of scientists to the notion that life could exist under seemingly inhospitable conditions on other planets" (Platt 1998). New studies may therefore take place in institutions such as NASA (National Aeronautics and Space Administration) and other world-renowned institutions. Furthermore, outside of these institutions, many individual scientists who are interested in the possible phenomenon of life in other solar systems have been pursuing their dream of one day discovering extraterrestrial life. However, we assume they are limited by the funds and technology that institutions have access to, and unless they are able to create an instrument that allows them to track down such planets, it is unlikely they will achieve their goal. Future studies at NASA involve studying the changes in Earth's chemical composition over billions of years. They will then apply this knowledge to other planets to look for chemical signatures that might indicate that life has existed or could exist there. And studies at NASA benefit the Origins Program's Terrestrial Planet Finder, which will look for Earth-like planets around other stars and hunt for signs of life-sustaining chemicals (Platt 1998). Astrobiological studies may prove valuable in the study of Jupiter's moon Europa, which may have liquid oceans under its frozen surface. This icy moon is currently being studied by NASA's Galileo Europa Mission, and a new Europa Orbiter had a launch planned for this year, 2003 (Lissauer 1999).

Conclusion

[20] We do not at present have enough information to determine the range of planetary systems that occur in nature. However, we do have a strong background of knowledge concerning the Universe, we know what we want to achieve, and we have ideas how to fulfill our desire. But we are unable to assemble the "what" and the "how" into something that will bring us the desired outcome. In other words, we are limited in our ability to use ambition to create instantaneously the technology needed to discover habitable planets. Nevertheless, our current understanding of the Universe drives us to explore the possibility of habitable planets. Much of the evidence over years of research is leaning toward the possibility that other planets exist with similar structure to that of the Earth. In fact, we have located these, planets that orbit stars as we on Earth orbit ours. It is only a matter of time before we will come across the technology to achieve our ultimate goal.

[21] I believe there is life on other planets; whether it is similar to that on Earth is yet to be determined. In addition, although it is taking science a great deal of time to produce the technology that will lead to new discoveries, I believe we have made tremendous breakthroughs concerning the evolution of the Universe. Humans have only been a part of the Universe an infinitesimal amount of time, but we are the ones teaching ourselves this fact.

[22] Let us leave with this final thought: there are billions of Sun-like stars in our galaxy; therefore, that there are planets containing life, whether similar or unlike that on Earth, is a realistic enough proposition. So that if we are never to detect other life forms in the Universe, technology is much more likely to be the principal limiting factor. Perhaps we, in our solar system, are found in a kind of Catch 22 situation. That is, we may be the only form of advanced life in the Universe able to ask questions about other planetary systems. Yet, because of our inability to create higher technology in order to discover other habitable planets, there may be other life-forms asking the question, "Is there intelligent life on Earth?"

References

Astrobiology: latest news signs of life. 2002. Retrieved Oct. 30, 2003 from the World Wide Web: http://astrobiology.arc.nasa.gov/news/expandnews.cfm?id=1204

Berrill, M. 2003, Oct. 27. The major transitions in the evolution of life. Lecture. Trent University, Peterborough.

The Canadian Institute for Advanced Research. 1987. Origin and evolution of the Universe: evidence for design? McGill-Queen's University Press, Kingston and Montreal.

Ducrocq, A. 1956. The origins of life. The Ryerson Press, Toronto.

Gupta, R.S. 1998. Life's third domain (Archaea): an established fact or an endangered paradigm?: a new proposal for classification of organisms based on protein sequences and cell structure. Theoretical Population Biol. 54: 91-104.

Hamilton, C.J. 2001. The solar system. Retrieved Oct. 24, 2003 from the World Wide Web: http://www.solarviews.com/eng/SOLARSYS.HTM

Hawking, S.W. 1988. A brief history of time: from the big bang to black holes. Bantam Books, New York.

Hughues, D.W. 1998. Wobbly pursuit of extrasolar planets. Nature 391: 651-652.

Kasting, J.F. 1996. Do other habitable planets exist and can we detect them? Astrophysics and Space Science 241: 3-24.

Kasting, J.F. 1997. Habitable zones around low mass stars and the search for extraterrestrial life. Origins of Life and Evolution of the Biosphere 27: 291-307.

Kasting, J.F., Whitmire, D.P., and Reynolds, R.T. 1993 Habitual zones around main sequence stars. Icarus 101: 108-128.

Lewis, J.S., and Prinn, R.G. 1984. Planets and their atmospheres: origin and evolution. Academic Press, Toronto.

Liebert, J., and Hubbard, W.B. 1999. Astronomy: big planets and little stars. Nature 400: 316-317.

Lissauer, J.J. 1999. Impacts of foreseeable science: how common are habitable planets? Nature 402: C11-C14.

Marcy, G. 1998. Extrasolar planets: back in focus. Nature 391: 127.

Moffat, S., and Shneour, E.A. 1986. Life beyond the earth. Scholastic Book Services, New York.

Ovenden, M.W. 1962. Life in the Universe: a scientific discussion. Anchor Books, New York.

Platt, J. 1998. JPL recruits two experts to hunt for new planets and life. Jet Propulsion Laboratory, California Institute of Technology, National Aeronautics and Space Administration. Retrieved Oct. 8, 2003 from the World Wide Web: http://www.jpl.nasa.gov/releases/98/quelneal.HTM

Sagan, C., and Shklovskii, I.S. 1966. Intelligent life in the Universe. Holden-Day, San Francisco.

Stebbins, G.L. 1969. The basis of progressive evolution. The University of North Carolina Press, Chapel Hill.

Sullivan, W. 1966. We are not alone: the search for intelligent life on other planets. The New American Library, New York.

The University of Michigan: University Corporation for Atmospheric Research. 2003. Windows to the Universe. Retrieved Oct. 20, 2003 from the World Wide Web: http://www.windows.ucar.edu/

Wetherill, G.W. 1995. The formation and habitability of extra-solar planets. Icarus **119**: 213-238.

Answer Key and Instructor's Guide

Chapter One
No exercises

Chapter Two — From Topic to Thesis
EXERCISE ONE: NARROWING THE TOPIC
This exercise works best with a group of students: each individual adds his or her own expertise about the topic at hand. Try narrowing each topic first for a 5000-word essay, then for a 2500-word essay.

EXERCISE TWO: RECASTING THE TOPIC IN QUESTION FORM
Try asking why, where, when, how, and who questions of each topic.

EXERCISE THREE: KEY WORDS AND CONCEPTS
Students should note the following key words:
1. negative, environmental, consequences, economic advantages, implementation, advanced technology, in relation to
2. commodification, virtue, modern
3. Treaty of Westphalia, Thirty Years' War, religious conflicts, Reformation, Counter-Reformation
4. methodological, Canadian settlement patterns, staples thesis, Innis, Creighton
5. world view, thematic reach, theatre of the absurd

EXERCISE FOUR: SUBDIVIDING THE TOPIC
1. This question is asking the student
   (a) to identify the values informing the UN's Earth Charter,
   (b) to judge its feasibility, and
   (c) to consider its possible effects.
   The student should use the questions as prompts for an essay in these three parts.
2. The overall question in this topic is the first instruction: discuss the social effects of the Industrial Revolution in Britain. The questions that follow are prompts to help the student explore the topic fully; they also suggest that a narrative approach would be appropriate.

EXERCISE FIVE: BREAKING UP THE TOPIC
1. Students might want to look at four specific changes, and then at how these changes have affected specific cities. Another possibility would be to look at one change in spatial patterns and to see how it manifested itself in a city from each region of Canada.

2. The student might want to decide on particular instances of "violence" and "cooperation" as foci and build the paper around them.

EXERCISE SIX: FINDING A POSITION
1. solar energy safer, nuclear cheaper; solar energy safer and cheaper; nuclear energy safer and cheaper; solar energy cheaper, nuclear safer
2. spanking always harmful and useless; spanking always harmless and useful; spanking sometimes harmless and useful; should become illegal; should be legal within clearly prescribed limits

EXERCISE SEVEN: BRAINSTORMING
No definite answers

EXERCISE EIGHT: FROM TOPIC TO THESIS STATEMENT
No definite answers

EXERCISE NINE: SAMPLE THESIS STATEMENTS
Note that, as is often the case in matters of essay writing, the sample thesis statements are not simply right or wrong. Some seriously flawed statements contain the germ of a good thesis; some strong statements could be improved upon.
1. Restates the topic (1)
2. Good cause-and-effect thesis statement; might be narrowed geographically to either Europe or North America (2)
3. Too broad (2); try narrowing each key concept in the statement
4. Basically a good statement but a bit wordy (4)
5. Restates the topic (1), and even as a topic is much too broad; as a self-evident proposition it fails the "so what" test (6, and most of the others as well)
6. In this form, "sensational" (5) and therefore not subject to proof; needs to be recast in the language of rational argument
7. Does not indicate central idea clearly (3) because reason and details given in second sentence are irrelevant to what is stated in first sentence
8. Wordy (4); condense to single sentence: "Bees communicate by performing dance-like motions that provide information about the direction and distance of nectar from the hive."
9. Strong statement: note "although" clause and clincher statement at the end
10. Strong statement
11. Cryptic (3). Is this a philosophy essay? a biology?
12. Too wordy (4); contains a reasonable argument but needs to be made more concise

198

13. Narrowly factual (5)
14. Strong statement
15. As stated, not subject to proof (5); recast in demonstrable form
16. Might be a good introductory statement, but not a thesis (1); thesis should go beyond statement to answer the question
17. Vague language; to an extent defines the prison in terms of itself ("caged mentally"); "frustrated lives" not explained adequately (3)

EXERCISE TEN: REFORMULATING THE THESIS
The essay claims the likelihood that life does exist on planets other than Earth but has not yet been discovered because of insufficiently advanced technology. The last sentence in the introduction should therefore state a stronger thesis, such as the following: More advanced technology, when it becomes available, would probably establish the existence of life on planets other than our own.

Chapter Three — Research
EXERCISE ONE: CHOOSING YOUR RESEARCH DIRECTION
1. Does demand research. Government documents useful; interviews with workers and management useful; documents developed by lobby groups and NGOs a good source; current books and articles. Problems: may be difficult to obtain government documents — some will be confidential; accessibility a problem with private sources as well; currency a problem since information in field is continually changing.
2. Does demand research. Read closely the texts of these authors and their biographies; consider secondary sources that evaluate these historians' works. Problems: time constraints — you will need to make choices about which primary texts to read.
3. Does demand research. Could look at books and articles on the subject, but statistical research would be more useful. Taxation laws might help. Problems: might be difficult to obtain necessary information from Statistics Canada; currency of information is an issue; masses of data to process; need to define "significant" in order to limit research.
4. Does demand research. Would need to look at lyrics of popular songs, musical theory, psychological studies of music. Problems: need to define "audience" (this might be tricky); problems with gauging popularity — different sources will use different indices.
5. Does not necessarily demand research — just lots of thinking. Student might want to look at by-laws, court rulings, etc.
6. Does not demand secondary research: student need only focus on *The Lost Salt Gift of Blood*.

Chapter Four — Reading

EXERCISE ONE: READING FOR DETAILED UNDERSTANDING

Instructors may find this a useful exercise at the beginning of term to encourage active reading.

EXERCISE TWO: READING FOR GENERAL KNOWLEDGE

This exercise works well as a classroom activity. The instructor can bring in a selection of books, give the students fifteen minutes to read them, and then ask each member of the class to report on what he or she has learned.

EXERCISE THREE: CRITICAL READING

Lots of room for discussion with this exercise. The initial task is to determine your own preference: which argument are you more sympathetic toward? Why? Students should look for unsupported generalizations. They should see that the first selection is strongly biased against any form of cloning and that the second attempts a balanced argument but, perhaps, sometimes overstates its case. In the first selection, they should note the author's reliance on ad hominem (personal-type) attacks on bioethicists, the medical-research industry, and the pharmaceutical industry. Then they can proceed to find instances of up-labelling ("one sensitive student") and down-labelling ("dirty little secret," "nonchalant"). In the second selection, students should look up scientific terms in a dictionary and then decide whether or not the author has employed these legitimately: does he need them to explain his ideas and make his case, or is he using them, or sometimes using them, just to make his argument sound more impressive because of the prestige of science? Then they can look for instances of figurative language ("lurid nightmares") and emotional appeal ("less than human") and decide whether these are justified by the argument or are over the top, that is, the first involving down-labelling and the second milking readers' sense of their humanity, to gain unfair argumentative advantage. The exercise can occupy up to an hour or more of classroom time with an enthusiastic class.

Chapter Five — Notetaking

EXERCISE ONE: NOTETAKING

1. Missing editors; not arranged in exact bibliographic order. Correct form: Hall, David J. "Clifford Sifton and Canadian Indian Administration, 1896-1905." *As Long as the Sun Shines and the Water Flows: A Reader in Canadian Native Studies*. Eds. Ian Getty and Antoine Lussier. Vancouver: U of British Columbia P, 1983. 132-46.
2. Paraphrasing is weak: large chunks are taken directly from original text. Note could cause student to plagiarize.

3. Fine, although Hall is not completely critical of Sifton's policies
4. Quotation is fine, but note is missing page number
5. Note needs to attribute information properly, both to Hall and to Sifton

EXERCISE TWO: PARAPHRASING
1. Fine, though not complete; no reference to the reasons for aid being offered
2. OK, although one might question whether the late 1950s means 1955-60
3. Not precise enough, especially in terms of dates
4. Sentence follows syntax of original too closely
5. Fine

EXERCISE THREE: PLAGIARISM
1. Depends too heavily on syntax from original source
2. Fine
3. Page reference should be cited
4. Fine

Chapter Six — Prewriting
EXERCISE ONE: FREE-WRITING
Good classroom exercise. Students may want to begin every writing session with a twenty-minute free-writing period.

EXERCISE TWO: METHODS OF ORGANIZATION
Try not to struggle for accuracy when doing this exercise; that will only slow you down. Make up ridiculous thesis statements — the Fathers of Confederation came together as a result of the moon being in Cancer — to see how you would use different methods of development to explore the thesis.

EXERCISE THREE: CREATING THE OUTLINE
For example, IV.2.a. could be modified in order to link discussion of the play's change in perspective more clearly to its adoption of Malvolio's point of view: As play progresses, perspective changes to Malvolio's.

EXERCISE FOUR: CONSTRUCTING THE REVERSE OUTLINE
1. No definite answer

2. **Sample Essay C in Appendix D** (numbers in square brackets refer to paragraphs)
Thesis: More advanced technology is needed . . . to prove the theory that there is life on other planets, and it is the lack of such technology

that limits us in our quest to make new discoveries about our Universe. (But see recommended thesis statement in the answer to Chapter Two, Exercise Ten.)

I. Comprehending magnitude and complexity of Universe requires understanding processes involved in its creation.
   1.   Big Bang theory
      a. zero size of Universe at 15 billion years ago;
      b. gradual cooling and formation of Universe *[2]*

   2.   illustration of scale proportions
      a. within our solar system;
      b. between our solar system and our galaxy *[3]*

II. Immensity of Universe and state of our sighting technology lead many scientists to believe that it is not reasonable to dismiss possibility of sustainable life on planets other than Earth.
   1.   immensity of Universe
      a. nearest star system to ours approximately four light years away;
      b. nearest galaxy to ours 2.2 million light years away

   2.   current telescopes not capable of clear detection at such distances *[4]*

III. Conditions for existence of life on a planet understood, but our cell-replication technology still prevents us from simulating them adequately.
   1.   conditions for existence of life
      a. Moscow conference; *[5]*
      b. Kasting et al. *[6]*

   2.   state of cell-replication experiments
      a. self-replicating cells created;
      b. created cells without genetic information *[6]*

IV. Understanding evolution of life on Earth would lead to understanding how life in distant galaxies may exist.
   1.   processes of evolution of life on Earth
      a. Earth's atmosphere, and creation and destruction of molecules resembling natural selection;
      b. protein;
      c. liquid water and presence of star like our Sun *[8]*

2. enabling temperatures
    a. discovery of archaebacteria in thermal heat vents;
    b. life may exist in forms previously unknown *[9]*

V. Importance of lower-mass stars for sustaining life.
    1. planets most likely to sustain life
        a. must have water;
        b. need lower-mass star like our Sun *[11]*

VI. Extrasolar planets: encouraging and discouraging discoveries.
    1. discovery of these planets
        a. planet orbiting 51 Pegasi;
        b. orbit so close to lower-mass star previously unimagined; *[14]*
        c. other planets *[15]*

    2. remaining unknowns but possibilities
        a. not yet come across planets with sustainable life;
        b. yet discovery of planets with "Suns" *[16]*

VII. Current and future studies: what's encouraging, undecided, or unknown.
    1. recent progress and problems in cosmology
        a. continual detection of new galaxies; *[17]*
        b. still insufficient agreement on defining life;
        c. problems regarding equipment sensitivity;
        d. problems of access to and analysis of extraterrestrial samples *[18]*

    2. good prospects of finding many more extrasolar planets
        a. great recent strides in technology;
        b. recent understanding of new life-sustaining conditions;
        c. studying changes in Earth's chemical composition over billions of years;
        d. applying knowledge on Earth's composition to detect chemical signatures on other planets *[19]*

It is possible to subsume section V within section IV by continuing the latter as follows:

3. planets most likely to sustain life
    a. must have water
    b. need a lower-mass star like our Sun *[11]*

Such subsumption may not seem like a big change, but, because of the continuity of the material in those sections, it can give the essay greater stride. Reduce the number of sections in an essay, and an outline, as much as possible to make the essay tighter. In this way you would also avoid giving the impression that you are walking on eggshells.

EXERCISE FIVE: CHECKING THE OUTLINE
Students should watch in particular for the method of development and the rhetorical arrangement used.

Chapter Seven — Drafting
No exercises

Chapter Eight — Revision
EXERCISE ONE: GENDER-NEUTRAL LANGUAGE
Several variations of the following answers are possible.
1. Narcissism represents the psychological dimension of this dependence. Notwithstanding occasional illusions of omnipotence, the validation of the self-esteem of narcissists depends on others. They cannot live without an admiring audience. Their apparent freedom from family ties and institutional constraints does not free them to stand alone or to glory in individuality. On the contrary, it contributes to insecurity, which they can overcome only by seeing their "grandiose self" reflected in the attentions of others, or by attaching themselves to those who radiate celebrity, power, and charisma. For narcissists, the world is a mirror, whereas the rugged individualist saw it as an empty wilderness to be shaped to his or her own design.
2. Being read fairy tales by a parent is one of the most enriching experiences in childhood. First, the mere presence of a parent is important. Reading is one of many ways in which special moments can be shared with the very young child. More important than the physical presence of parents is the role they play as mediator between the child and the fairy story. A mother or father makes a child feel safe in the presence of giants, hungry wolves, and wicked stepsisters. Yet there is an even more subtle kind of reassurance given to the child by the reading parent. Psychologists tell us that the basis of most fears in

early childhood is the child's emerging independence from, and subsequent guilt about, his or her parents. By being present as children imaginatively kill off wicked stepmothers and replace them with Prince Charmings, parents can indicate to children that indulging in fantasies of independence is acceptable. Children can be assured that Mom and Dad will survive these aggressive fantasies, and respond to that simultaneous need to be dependent.

EXERCISE TWO: THE HISTORICAL PRESENT

Try changing the historical present to the past in the final paragraph of Sample Essay A and the second-last paragraph of Sample Essay B. Then compare these revised paragraphs with the originals for effectiveness. In the first two paragraphs of the "Extrasolar Planets" section in Sample Essay C, decide in which sentences it would have been better to use the simple present.

EXERCISE THREE: PARAGRAPH STRUCTURE AND
THE CONTROLLING IDEA

1. **Controlling Idea**: "There were three groups which caused the weakening of the Shah's position."
   Methods of Organization: classification, some cause and effect, general to specific
   Devices for Coherence: parallel structure ("First there were . . . Second there were . . . Then there were . . ." and "Some sided . . . Others sided . . . Still others were dedicated . . ."), transitional devices (adding ideas: first, second, then; summary words: group, middle class)
2. **Controlling Idea**: "Industrial wastes are upsetting nature's balance in every region of this country."
   Methods of Organization: description, specific to general
   Devices for Coherence: parallel structure ("In . . . In . . . In . . .")
3. **Controlling Idea**: "Beneath the epidermis lies a much thicker portion of the skin — the dermis."
   Methods of Organization: description, general to specific
   Devices for Coherence: pronouns (it, this)
4. **Controlling Idea**: "The Potlatch Law was difficult to enforce."
   Methods of Organization: narration
   Devices for Coherence: transitional devices (then, however), repeated words (potlatch, law)

EXERCISE FOUR: PARAGRAPH STRUCTURE AND TRANSITIONS WITHIN PARAGRAPHS

Compare your version to the first paragraph in Sample Essay A. Note how simple words like "but" and "these" can make the connections clearer and therefore the transitions smoother.

EXERCISE FIVE: PARAGRAPH STRUCTURE AND TRANSITIONS WITHIN PARAGRAPHS

Paragraph one: it would help to insert "however" in the last sentence, to make clear that this sentence expresses a reservation concerning the view represented in the previous sentence.

Paragraph two: it would help to insert "but" or "yet" at the beginning of the fourth sentence, to make clear that a contrast is being expressed in relation to what the previous sentence states.

Paragraph three: inserting any of "but," "yet," "however," "nevertheless," "at the same time" or "even so" in the second sentence would help to make clear the contrast between this sentence and the one before it.

EXERCISE SIX: INCORPORATING QUOTATIONS IN PARAGRAPHS

1. Quotation is incorporated well. Student introduces significance of quotation, quotes, and then explains quotation.
2. Slightly confusing. The connection between the quotation and the comment about Nigeria is not sufficiently explained. Student needs to show that Africa, Nigeria, and Biafra can all be considered nations, depending on how the term "nation" is defined.
3. Quotation is incorporated well. In particular, the way in which the student has made reference to the quotation in the sentences that follow it is effective.
4. First quotation is nicely introduced but not explained well enough in the comments that follow it. The result is that the two quotations seem strung together.

EXERCISE SEVEN: TRANSITIONS BETWEEN PARAGRAPHS

Paragraph five: A transitional phrase, such as "in contrast" or "in contrast to liberal democracy," would facilitate a reader's passage from paragraph four.

Paragraph ten: beginning this paragraph with a word like "for," or a partial repetition like "these conflicts would occur because," might ease a reader's passage from paragraph nine.

EXERCISE EIGHT: INTRODUCTIONS

1. Strong introduction that gives background leading to thesis; thesis turns on interesting irony

2. Weak, apologetic introduction that has no thesis and dissolves into confused, illogical, and unrelated details
3. Background, defining terms; thesis is clarified by a contrast between the author's view and that of other writers
4. Controversial quotation with which the author disagrees; effective introduction
5. Too broad, too vague, and undermines the essay
6. Contains a reasonable thesis, but as an introduction is inadequately developed to capture the interest of the reader
7. Empty appreciation of literary work; logical problem with "but" transition; disjointed, inadequate development with only a vague articulation of a possible thesis
8. Too broad; each of the four sentences could be the subject of its own essay
9. Uses question format to define problems and find solutions; workable as long as the essay lives up to the introduction
10. Weak, apologetic, personal, naive-sounding

EXERCISE NINE: CONCLUSIONS
1. Merely restates the thesis; uses stock phrases
2. Effective conclusion; restates thesis in interesting way and widens scope to consider possible solutions to problem that essay has defined
3. Uses anecdote effectively to illustrate complex thesis
4. Begins with clear statement of thesis, but ends with an analogy so loose that instead of widening the scope, it jumps the track into an unrelated area; try to imagine an analogy that would work better, one that would clearly show the modern knowledge derived from basic research
5. Empty appreciation unrelated to topic of the essay
6. Effective conclusion that widens scope as with a telephoto lens to put problem in a larger context
7. Unnecessarily apologetic; weak
8. Effective summing up of problem along with suggested solutions
9. Effective use of biographical anecdote to cap essay
10. Essay derailed at the last moment by an afterthought that is irrelevant to the major concerns of the essay

EXERCISE TEN: INTRODUCTIONS AND CONCLUSIONS
Wilkes introduction and conclusion work well because they follow the same thesis but express that thesis differently; progressive movement conclusion is too much a restatement of introduction; introduction and conclusion on school closures work well because conclusion answers questions posed in introduction.

EXERCISE ELEVEN: INTRODUCTIONS AND CONCLUSIONS

Sample Essay A: Introduction (first paragraph) clear and to the point but, after the first three lead-in sentences, could gather up the thesis into one succinct statement. Conclusion (last paragraph) fine.

Sample Essay B: Introduction (first two paragraphs) a little too long. Could be more concise by combining the last sentence of the first paragraph and the last two sentences of the second paragraph in a single thesis statement. Conclusion (last two paragraphs) is strong in that it reinforces and expands on solutions to problems the essay has raised, but it goes on for too long and therefore has the effect of continuing the discussion rather than closing it.

Sample Essay C: Introduction (first paragraph) well developed but needs a stronger thesis statement (last sentence) to match the essay's argument better. Conclusion (last three paragraphs) strong in that it reinforces the argument with a rational imaginative appeal and at the same time shows appropriate caution.

EXERCISE TWELVE: REVISING SYNTAX THROUGH COORDINATION AND SUBORDINATION

These sentences can be combined in a variety of ways. One possibility for each of the sentences is listed below.

1. Nuclear power is not only costly, but it also produces potentially deadly wastes that, as of yet, we do not know how to dispose of.
2. When North American Native People suffered from sicknesses, they recognized these sicknesses as European and therefore would often accept European remedies.
3. I saw a wild hog foraging in the woods, its face covered with mud; it reminded me of my brother eating spaghetti.
4. After having spent millions of dollars on research, car manufacturers have developed small-horsepower engines that will travel twice as far on a gallon of gas as today's engines.
5. Scientists have a difficult role because, while they must be aware of the advantages of their discoveries, they must be equally aware of the disadvantages.

EXERCISE THIRTEEN: REVISING SYNTAX BY EMPLOYING PARALLEL STRUCTURE

Parallel structure can be fun: play around with these sentences. Answers will vary.

EXERCISE FOURTEEN: REVISING DICTION

1. Short choppy sentences all of the same length and construction; no connections between ideas to indicate relative importance or logical relationships
2. Computerese that may be appropriate to certain technical contexts within the computer world, but comes across as vague, wooden, stilted jargon in the outside world
3. Clear writing; note the precision of this phrasing, its parallel structure and precise logical relationships
4. Self-conscious over-writing; note the overuse of nouns, unnecessary modifiers, and their usual companions, weak verb forms
5. Too casual for rigorous thought or intelligent reader

EXERCISE FIFTEEN: REVISING DICTION

The original paragraph was deliberately exaggerated to show the leaps of logic that could occur when an author uses generalizations instead of concrete words. The following revision establishes the author's line of reasoning more precisely and indeed makes clear the illogicalities of that reasoning.

Both Macbeth and Lady Macbeth share a desire for power more than any other human goal. Although Lady Macbeth seems to persuade Macbeth to commit murder, in fact, both want to accomplish the grisly deed. However, after Duncan has been slain, Macbeth sees ghosts and his wife thinks she cannot wash Duncan's blood from her hands. Finally, the predictions of the witches come true and Macbeth is killed. Hamlet, too, is incited to murder, but he is indecisive about taking such action against Claudius. King Lear was like the Macbeths in that he wanted power, or, more precisely, he wanted power back. Power is also a problem in *Othello*, although one of narrower scope, since Othello primarily wants control over his wife, not a kingdom. This discrepancy in scope has led a few critics to believe that it was Francis Bacon who wrote about the Moor of Venice.

EXERCISE SIXTEEN: REVISING GRAMMAR

No particular answer.

EXERCISE SEVENTEEN: REVISING GRAMMAR

To "sum" an existence, "bound" a life, and find safety in the "strait limits" of an enclosed mind — this *was* the motive of the fictional autobiographers of Charlotte Brontë's novels. All three autobiographers ["Because" omitted] seem to need to oversimplify both their own natures and the worlds in which they live [second "in" omitted]. They are all different; however, *their methods are* basically the same [exclamation mark omitted]. Repressing what *their* more instinctual impulses tell *them* about the complex truths of experience, [words omitted] they generate personal mythologies by which to rationalize their lives.

EXERCISE EIGHTEEN: PROOFREADING

Roughing It in the Bush, Susanna Moodie's witty and moving book about her experiences in Upper Canada during the 1830s, seems to capture the essence of Canadian life. However, were it not for the storytelling skills of another writer, our beloved Susanna might never have come to Canada. Susanna's husband Dunbar filled his book *Ten Years in South Africa* with so many tales of danger and mishap that Susanna emphatically refused to accompany him to so terrifying and dangerous a country. It was unfortunate for the Moodies that Dunbar wrote so convincingly — they undoubtedly would have fared better there than they did in Canada.

Index

NOTES

NOTES